21-DAY DEVOTIONAL:
GOD'S PERFECT TIMING JOURNAL

Companion Bible Study & Daily Reflections
Through the Book of Ruth

Prayer Prompts, Grace Tracker & Journaling Pages

AF374114

Susie J. Owens

For Daniel, who saw the book in me before I did. And for his repeated mantra, "Mom, just finish the book."

And for my son Zach and his incredible young friends (Liv, Ashley, Josh, Lucas, Matt, and Kit)—thank you for keeping me on my toes and demanding the next chapters!

21-Day Devotional: God's Perfect Timing: A Guided Prayer Journal & Bible Study Through the Book of Ruth
Copyright © 2025 by Susie J. Owens

…He Comes to Us Like Rain
They meant it as a question, but I took
it as a dare. Mom, have you ever read
the Bible all the way through?

After picking a one-year plan, and
five years later, I finished reading
every word of the Holy Bible. New
Living Translation.

I was so profoundly struck by the
beauty of the words; the intimacy
they offer us with Almighty God.

This book is meant to nudge you to
open a Bible and start your own
journey to finding your own special
"spring rain."

"Let us acknowledge the Lord; let us
press on to acknowledge him. As
surely as the sun rises, he will appear;
he will come to us like the winter
rains, like the spring rains that water
the earth." (Hosea 6:3).

TABLE OF CONTENTS

Grab your free Divine Timing by susiej.com/timing, or scan this QR code

INTRODUCTION:
YOUR STORY IS ALREADY IN MOTION

A Gift for You
Your Free Gift: The Personal Divine
Timing Evidence Log

You are holding Ruth's story in your hands right now, but what about yours?

God is writing a beautiful story in your life right now—and this free tool will help you see it clearly. The free Divine Timing Evidence Log will help you:

- Recognize where you are in your faith journey today.

- Celebrate how God has already been working in your life.

- Discover what He may have planned for your next season.

- Pray with clarity and gratitude.

The Log includes the Seven Stations of Divine Timing. Whether you are in the "Gleaning Field" of hard work or the "Threshing Floor" of risky faith, knowing where you are changes how you pray and the way you live.

Grab your personal copy of the Divine Timing Tracker @ susiej.com/timing, or by scanning this QR Code.

Help More Readers Find This Book!

If you are enjoying this book, would you consider leaving a review? Sometimes the hardest part is knowing what to say. Here are a few prompts to get your started:

I liked this book because….

This book helped me see…..

I bought this book for …. Because…..

I'm glad I bought this book because….

Just scan this QR code to be taken directly to the review page. Thanks so much.

A FREE GIFT FOR YOU

Your Personal Divine Timing
Evidence Log

You are holding Ruth's story in your hands right now, but what about yours?

God is writing a beautiful story in your life right now—and this free tool will help you see it clearly.

The Divine Timing Evidence Log helps you:

Recognize where you are in your faith journey today.
Celebrate how God has already been working in your life.
Discover what He may have planned for your next season.
Pray with clarity and gratitude.

Inside you'll find the Seven Stations of Divine Timing—a framework based on Ruth's journey from loss to redemption.

The Log includes the Seven Stations of Divine Timing. Whether you are in the "Gleaning Field" of hard work or the "Threshing Floor" of risky faith, knowing where you are changes how you pray and the way you live.

Grab your personal copy of the
Divine Timing Tracker @
susiej.com/timing

DAY 1: RUTH 1:1-3

In the days when the judges ruled, there was a famine in the land, and a man from Bethlehem in Judah, together with his wife and two sons, went to live in the land of Moab for a while. The man's name was Elimelech, his wife's name was Naomi, and the names of his two sons were Mahlon and Chilion. They were Ephrathites from Bethlehem in Judah. And they entered the land of Moab and settled there. Then Naomi's husband Elimelech died, and she was left with her two sons (BSB)

How long does it take for a person to lose their way? How long before drifting feels normal, before the turn is so slight you don't notice you're walking in the wrong direction? Unraveling rarely arrives as a single event. It arrives undetected, one thread at a time.

In this story, it is a logical, but unwise, decision that undoes a life stitch by stitch. And while the book is called Ruth, this story doesn't begin with her at all. Instead, it starts with a famine; the kind that cracks the earth like old pottery and makes hope as dry as dust. Hunger takes root. Fear grows beside it, and it drives men to make choices they believe are responsible, even faithful. And this is where we find Elimelek, standing in soil so starved that it forgets how to cradle a seed. So, he decides to gather his life, his wife, and his sons, and leave Bethlehem, the "house of bread."

Across the Jordan is Moab. There, the fields are green. Bread rises in ovens with a scent that promises Elimelek more than just survival, but comfort. Elimelek, whose name really means, My God is King, only intends for the move to be temporary. The Hebrew text uses the word *gur*—a brief sojourn. Just until the famine breaks. Surely God will understand.

But Elimelek knows Moab. He knows its worship is marked by fear, its altars stained red by child sacrifice. He knows its origins are tangled with the wreckage after Sodom's destruction. And yet this is where Elimelek takes his wife, Naomi, and their sons. A hint of what's to come is hidden in the sons' names: Mahlon means *sickness*, and Kilion means *destruction*.

Days fold into weeks. Weeks into years. A full decade passes. The man named "My God Is King" no longer lives as though God is King. The unraveling completes itself, and ten years after he leaves the land where God is King, he dies in soil that was never meant to receive his bones. In ancient times, to be buried outside the covenant land was to be severed from your ancestors, from the long legacy of your own people. To be forgotten. Now, Elimelek's unraveling is complete.

There's a way that seems right but leads to death, as Proverbs 14:12 teaches. The path that initially looks promising but ultimately ends in disappointment. This is what happens when God's people forsake the spring of living water and dig their own cisterns—broken cisterns that cannot hold water, as Jeremiah warns (Jeremiah 2:13).

But in Bethlehem, a different story is unfolding. Boaz, a kinsman of Elimelek, stays. Same famine. Same hunger. Different choice. The earth cracks under his feet, too, but he stays. And somehow, thrives.

Elimelek fled famine, hoping to preserve his life; yet the path he chose cost him everything. Boaz endures the famine because he trusts the God who governs the famine. His strength is not rooted in barns or calculations but in the One who commands the rain.

DIVINE TIMING INSIGHT

Elimelek fled famine. Boaz stayed through it. And divine timing reveals why that difference mattered. But here's what divine timing reveals: staying wasn't just about geography; it was about preparation. While Elimelek wandered for ten years, Boaz was being shaped into the man who could redeem what Elimelek would leave broken. God was positioning the kinsman-redeemer before the widow ever needed one.

TRACING YOUR OWN THREADS OF DIVINE TIMING

"There is a way that appears to be right, but in the end it leads to death." (Proverbs 14:12)

What does the world think is best for me, and is it the same as what God wants for me? Am I running, or am I being wise?

"For the revelation awaits an appointed time... Though it linger, wait for it; it will certainly come and will not delay." (Habakkuk 2:3)

How do I tend to fill the gap between God's promise and God's timing—with faith or with fear?

"He has made everything beautiful in its time." (Ecclesiastes 3:11)

Where have I mislabeled something as "wasted" that God is actually calling "in process"?

"Be patient, then, brothers and sisters, until the Lord's coming... Be patient and stand firm." (James 5:7–8)

What foundation am I standing on—fear, control, or trust?

FILL-IN REFLECTION

What choice have I made that seemed wise at the time but now feels like a mistake?

____

____

____

____

If God is already near in that broken place, what might He be preparing that I cannot yet see?

____

____

____

____

____

____

What part of my life feels cracked or thinning, where the ground feels like it's shifting beneath me?

DAY 2: RUTH 1:4-5

They took Moabite wives, one named Orpah and the other Ruth. And after they had lived there about ten years, both Mahlon and Chilion also died, and Naomi was left without her two sons and her husband (BSB)

Elimelek promised Naomi a temporary stay; just a brief sojourn until the famine passes. But ten years unfurl beneath Moab's sun, and this is how temporary becomes permanent, how compromise hardens into habit, how the unfamiliar begins to feel like home.

A decade can do a lot. It blurs the road back, making it harder to remember where you came from. The place you swore you'd return to doesn't feel like home anymore; it almost feels farther away than the place from which you've been running. It's long enough for your sons to marry women whose gods feel unfamiliar, and for your roots to sink deep into soil that was never meant to hold your family's future.

The weddings of Naomi's sons should have brought flashes of hope weaving through her grief: a growing household, the promise of grandchildren. But each wedding is another cord binding Naomi to a land God never intended for her to be in. Ten years. Long enough for exile to dress itself in the clothing of destiny. Long enough for the heart to settle where it is never meant to take root.

But then both sons die, and even more crucially, they die without children. The dire implications are immediate and total: no husband, no sons, no male heirs.

But God has woven multiple safety nets into the Law for situations like this. In Leviticus 25:25-55, God created the kinsman-redeemer system—the go'el—where a near relative could buy back family land sold due to poverty, ensuring the family's inheritance remained intact. In Deuteronomy 25:5-10, God instituted levirate marriage, requiring a brother to marry his deceased brother's widow if they had been living together and the brother died childless. This ensured the widow would not lose her place in the family and that her dead husband's name would continue through offspring.

But Naomi's situation is even more catastrophic than either law was designed to address. Her nearest male relatives are dead—there are no brothers to fulfill levirate obligations. The kinsman-redeemer law allows relatives to buy back land, but it says nothing about protecting widows or requiring marriage. Naomi has no husband to claim the land, no sons to inherit it, and no clear legal path to restoration. At the moment her sons die, Naomi loses:

her land (which could only be held through male heirs),

her income,

her legal standing,

and her protection within the community.

Without a husband or sons, Naomi (whose name ironically means pleasant) has become legally invisible—functionally dead within the system. She is stripped of every thread that once held her life together. Far away in Moab, Naomi is a woman disconnected from the one system designed to anchor and sustain her. She has no place left in the world to lay her head. In ancient Israel, Naomi has become untethered from the legal system that could anchor her.

But what if Orpah and Ruth did remarry? Moabite husbands, new households, and maybe even grandchildren? Even if the women took Moabite husbands, these men—as foreigners— would have no legal standing in Bethlehem to redeem Naomi's land or restore Elimelek's family line.

Naomi would be an outsider to these new unions. Her 'grandchildren' would carry none of Naomi's bloodline. They would be raised to worship Chemosh rather than Yahweh. Naomi, already alone without her husband and sons, would remain stranded in a foreign land, forever cut off from her people and her God.

In the midst of this darkness, a question hovers above her. And it's the same question that haunts you: Why Naomi? Why should she be left to suffer the consequences of choices she never made? *If only* Elimelek had never brought her here. *If only* her sons had given her grandsons. *If only* she had one more son, still alive.

Why should Naomi, the innocent, be left to suffer? Why would God allow this hopelessness?

The answer lies within the Hebrew text. A single word that has multiple meanings in English: "Vatisha'er," from the root "sha'ar." This word means to remain. To be left behind. To survive. "Sha'ar" is the word for remnant, the portion preserved, held back for something that is still unfolding. It is not punishment. It is preservation.

These are the same words used to describe Noah when the waters swallowed the earth. "Only Noah remains alive." "Vayisha'er akh Noach." Noah, not punished, preserved. Saved. Spared. He is preserved.

The same words are used here for Naomi. Not punished, preserved. And here's something else she can't see yet. God is *releasing* her. She's being released from the bad decisions that were made for her, the ones that dragged her across the countryside ten years ago, into the cursed land of Moab. She is far from being abandoned and left for dead; God is reaching down to save her. Not cursed and not forgotten, but held by the God who sees the last ember even when the fire appears gone. She is left. "Vatisha'er."

But now, there's a new question rising, like smoke from embers cooling down: How? How can God restore a life that's been stripped bare? How does He redeem someone who's too old to start over, too wounded to dream of anything beyond surviving?

In this story, as with all the great stories in the Bible, God's timing is perfect. He's never late—He is orchestrating. From what's left, from the remnants, from the seed that appears dead beneath the soil, heaven descends. God will weave His plan into everyday moments, aligning chaos into order, opening doors to redemption. Yes. Naomi's arms are empty, but this is precisely where God makes room. She can't see it yet, but she isn't abandoned. From this devastation, she'll receive honor and praise that stretches across nations.

DIVINE TIMING INSIGHT

Throughout Scripture, we see the same architecture: God brings loss, then abundance. Noah's flood washes the world clean before remaking it. Job loses everything, then receives twice what he had. Abraham lifts the knife over his son, and from that moment of total surrender, nations are born. The pattern holds: emptiness first, then overflow. A pattern becomes clear: God subtracts before He multiplies. He empties before He fills. He clears away what can't stay, so we can make room for what He intends to give. Sometimes, He even lets what we've built in the wrong place collapse, creating space for something truer to take its place.

TRACING YOUR OWN THREADS OF DIVINE TIMING

"Only Noah remained." (Genesis 7:23)
> When have I lost something and thought it was devastation, only to find it was actually deliverance?

"The Lord is close to the brokenhearted." (Psalm 34:18)
> Do I close God out from my pain, or do I let Him in to walk with me?

"I will restore the years the locusts have eaten." (Joel 2:25)
> If I look back, can I see that God has given me blessings that I take for granted?

FILL-IN REFLECTION

There are dreams I once held close. Dreams of:

____

____

____

____

But then everything shifted: I lost:

____

____

I thought I would find:

____

____

____

____

But instead, I found:

____

____

____

Maybe being left is not a curse. Maybe it is:

____

____

____

____

____

____

____

____

____

DAY 3: RUTH 1:6-7

When Naomi heard in Moab that the LORD had attended to His people by giving them food, she and her daughters-in-law prepared to return from the land of Moab. So she left the place where she had been living, accompanied by her two daughters-in-law, and they set out on the road that would take them back to the land of Judah (BSB)

Naomi stands in Moab, the land east of Judah, where the rains have fallen, and the fields are green, but with a heart still sick with grief. Now, she hears that there is food again in Bethlehem.

Notice that the text does not say the famine ended. Instead, it says, "…the Lord had come to the aid of His people by providing food for them…" (Ruth 1:6). Here, provision is not presented as some random chance, a break in the weather, but as a purposeful intention, provided by God. For his people. As mercy. Rain falls in Bethlehem, and with rain, bread.

During drought, plants release oils into the soil, and bacteria settle into the dust. When the first drops of rain finally arrive, those hidden elements mix and react, and release geosmin, and a fragrance blooms on the earth. Petrichor. It's a scent perfumers strive to emulate. Divine timing works like this, too: silent stratums forming beneath the surface, unseen and unhurried, until the precise moment they are stirred, they become visible. The fragrance of earth remembering rain.

The Lord has visited His people, so Naomi prepares to move. For Naomi, it is God's "…teaching falling like rain and words descending like dew" (Deuteronomy 32:2). The text tells us she prepared for the journey, gathering, sorting through what remains after loss has taken so much, deciding what stays and what must be left behind.

The news came, not with a celestial sign, a thunderbolt, or an angel pointing east. Naomi doesn't wait for extraordinary signs when God is already speaking through simple ones. No command to go. Only a whisper of opportunity; rain is falling, bread is baking. Naomi does not know what awaits her in Bethlehem. She only knows that the famine is over, and she cannot remain where her hope has died.

It's too easy, sometimes, to stay in the place you never meant to stay, especially when life has been heavy. It's hard to move, easy to defer, to wait for perfect certainty. Because hoping comes at too high a price, sometimes. Hope becomes a dare. But for Naomi, the greatest danger to her soul is not the grief of her losses, but staying lost when the door to return home is open. The longer she remains in a wounded place, the more bitterness can settle in like stone.

Two unlikely companions walk beside her. By every cultural, religious, and national measure, they should stand on opposite sides of a long and complicated history. These women owe her nothing. Their legal bond to Naomi ended when Mahlon and Kilion were buried beneath Moab's soil. They could stay; they should stay. Remarry, step back into familiar customs and warm kitchens, and the safety of their mothers' households. Rebuild lives that make sense on Moabite terms, free from the sorrow of following a widow who has nothing left to offer except her own grief.

But these women have watched Naomi bury a husband and two sons, and they might be a bit intrigued by what holds her together after such loss. They have seen Naomi cling to the God of Israel in the darkness, even when reason says she shouldn't. They have seen her sit in the dust of mourning, whispering to a God they do not know, clinging to Him as her world collapses. Something in that stubborn attachment has shaped them. It has carved questions into their hearts. Naomi has introduced them to covenant love. Hesed. A love that remains true even when a world falls apart.

Naomi begins walking toward home. Restoration sometimes begins not with miracles but with movement, not with certainty but with willingness. God provides the rain. Naomi chooses the road.

So, they walk. Three widowed women on a dusty road. One Hebrew. Two Moabites. All grieving. All uncertain. All carrying the weight of their losses with a faint shimmer of possibility. They gather what little they have and turn their faces toward Judah.

Naomi has heard the news. Bread is rising in the House of Bread. Rain is falling. Grain is pushing through soil that once crumbled at the touch. There is nothing left for her in Moab. But maybe something waits for her in Bethlehem. Even if it's simply the dignity of returning home to die among her own people, under the care of the God she cannot stop believing in, even when He feels silent.

But God is already ahead of her. Naomi doesn't know it yet. He's already organizing, preparing, and aligning people and events for her arrival.

DIVINE TIMING INSIGHT

"…he will come to us like the winter rains, like the spring rains that water the earth" (Hosea 6:3). He arranges our provision out of sight, setting answers in place before we ever become aware of them. The rain and the scent of petrichor are a reminder of the invisible hand of grace, working beneath the surface so that everything arrives at its appointed time. We can't see this happening, but long before the rain, a thirsty plant and soil work together, waiting in silence beneath the earth. When the first rain finally falls, what was hidden rises, creating that sweet, familiar, earthy scent. Divine timing works this way.

TRACING YOUR OWN THREADS OF DIVINE TIMING

"Let us acknowledge the Lord; let us press on to acknowledge him. As surely as the sun rises, he will appear; he will come to us like the winter rains, like the spring rains that water the earth." (Hosea 6:3)

Do I live as if God's presence is as sure as the sunrise— or do I still doubt His nearness?

"The Lord was not in the wind… not in the earthquake… not in the fire.
And after the fire came a gentle whisper." (1 Kings 19:11–12)

Am I waiting for thunder, earthquakes, or divine signs when I could start taking the reasonable steps God has already placed right in front of me?

"May he be like rain falling on a mown field, like showers watering the earth." (Psalm 72:6)

Where are my petrichor moments? The places that I can now point to, and see that God was one step ahead, providing and preparing the way?

FILL-IN REFLECTION

I notice a change beginning when:

____

____

____

The thing that has shifted or unraveled is:

____

____

____

God may be nudging me through this small mercy:

____

____

____

The choice I can make today is:

____

____

____

____

What I am waiting for—and what may be holding me still:

DAY 4: RUTH 1:8-10

Then Naomi said to her two daughters-in-law, "Go back, each of you, to your mother's home. May the LORD show you loving devotion, as you have shown to your dead and to me. May the LORD grant that each of you will find rest in the home of another husband." And she kissed them as they wept aloud and said to her, "Surely we will go back with you to your people" (BSB)

Somewhere between Moab to the east and Bethlehem to the west, not fully belonging to one place and not yet arriving at the other, lies the landscape of transition. It is here—in this in-between stretch—where the past stays visible behind the three widows, and the future waits with unknown edges ahead. It is here that Naomi stops walking.

Now that the steady repetition of putting one foot in front of the other has cleared her mind, she begins to think. She knows the law is clear: "No Ammonite or Moabite or any of their descendants may enter the assembly of the LORD, not even in the tenth generation" (Deuteronomy 23:3). The realization of the shame these women could face in Bethlehem might be the catalyst that urges both to go back.

Wisdom often appears fragile. It looks like choosing honesty when you would rather pretend things will be easy. Naomi knows the truth. She could keep walking and let Ruth and Orpah follow her all the way to Bethlehem. She could let their loyalty carry them forward without warning. But she can't do this to them. Naomi understands what awaits them there: Poverty. Hard labor. The disgrace of being widowed Moabites in a town that may not welcome them.

In her words, she does not say, "to your father's house," which is the usual phrase. She chooses, instead, the words, "mother's home." She, mercifully, knows fathers may not welcome back childless widowed daughters with open arms, but mothers might see survival instead of loss. Naomi is not casting them aside. She is telling the truth. She releases her daughters because she loves them.

The word "kindness," which appears twice in Ruth 1:8, can be translated as the Hebrew word "hesed."

"Hesed." Covenant love. A love that holds fast when logic says to let go. Love that endures when no one is watching. Hesed is the way God loves His people. It is what makes Him promise, "I will betroth you to me forever" in Hosea 2:19. And Naomi has seen it in these two women. They were not required to stay with her after Mahlon and Kilion died. No tradition compelled them. Yet they stayed. Shared her grief. Looked after her. Walked beside her when they were free to walk away.

Now Naomi is giving the two women the blessing of hesed in return. Even in her emptiness, even when she cannot imagine God being kind to her again, she can still ask God to be kind to them. This is faith that remains alive in the smallest embers.

"May the Lord grant that each of you will find rest in the home of another husband." The word "rest" here in Hebrew is "menuchah." Rest. Stability. A place to stand without fear. A home where one is known and sheltered.

Naomi blesses the women, even though she knows so much loss right now. She kisses them goodbye, the kiss of someone who has nothing to offer except truth and therefore offers truth as her act of love. They break into tears. Three women standing between two worlds, each tasting grief, each feeling the cost of loyalty.

But these daughters have seen that through her sorrow, Naomi's faith bends but does not break. They have watched her grieve in darkness, and even through the anger that grief brings, she has not turned away from her God. Ruth and Orpah answer with a resolve that surprises even Naomi. "We will go back with you to your people." Love that defies logic. Hesed answering hesed.

Naomi blesses even while bitter. She invokes the name of the Lord even when she wonders if He still hears her. Naomi grieves, but she does not abandon Yahweh. The daughters watch this, and it leaves them, at first, with no other choice but to follow her. Ruth and Orpah have learned covenant love by seeing it in Naomi's life.

DIVINE TIMING INSIGHT

Sometimes love asks you to let go of what you cherish. Sometimes, faithfulness asks you to let go of what cannot be held on to. Naomi chooses honesty instead of persuasion. She names the cost of following her and blesses Ruth and Orpah with freedom rather than guilt. Only one choice will carry the legacy. Only one carries hesed.

TRACING YOUR OWN THREADS OF DIVINE TIMING

"Who knows but that you have come to your royal position for such a time as this?" (Esther 4:14)

> In the midst of my own losses, have I ever considered that God has work for me to do? Am I showing up for others in a way that reflects and honors God?

"Carry each other's burdens, and in this way you fulfill the law of Christ."(Galatians 6:2)

> Am I willing to sacrifice convenience or comfort to love someone well?

"Walk in the way of love, just as Christ loved us and gave himself up for us…" (Ephesians 5:2)

> What fear, pride, or habit keeps me from giving myself entirely in love the way Christ did?

FILL-IN REFLECTION

What quality would I like to embody to love like Christ?

____

____

____

____

What kind of love is Christ forming in me?

____

____

____

Today, I could ask for God's help with

DAY 5: RUTH 1:11-13

But Naomi replied, "Return home, my daughters. Why would you go with me? Are there still sons in my womb to become your husbands? Return home, my daughters; go on your way, for I am too old to have another husband. Even if I thought there was hope for me, even if I had a husband tonight and bore sons, would you wait until they grew up? Would you refrain from having husbands? No, my daughters. It is much more bitter for me than for you, because the LORD's hand has gone out against me" (BSB)

Naomi walks west toward Bethlehem; the grief of the events in Moab is still folded inside her. Her feet move toward the land of promise, but her heart has not crossed the border. Tears fall into the dust, and something inside of Naomi breaks.

Her words have not moved the women yet, and now what escapes her mouth is not the gentle nudging she used before. This time, she paints the bleakest picture possible, trying to spare Ruth and Orpah from a future that looks like ruin.

Naomi lays out the harshness of life before them, creating a scenario with almost dark humor. Even if she married tonight, even if sons were born by morning, would they wait decades for boys to become men? She has used up every strategy, and there is no rescue plan or future she can offer them.

"It is more bitter for me than for you, for the Lord's hand has turned against me." She names this new conclusion about herself, one that has been justly earned and has shaped everything she says and does. A theology sculpted by pain rather than truth. She believes what Deuteronomy 28 warns, that the same covenant hand that brings blessing to obedience can bring hardship to disobedience, and she assumes she is living under its shadow. She believes she has been singled out, marked, quietly rejected by the God she once trusted. Not to hurt Ruth and Orpah, but to try to protect them from becoming versions of her.

Naomi's bitterness is not rebellion. It is a lament that has been sealed too long. Scripture is full of such voices. Job cries, "The hand of God has struck me" (Job 19:21). Elijah whispers, "I have had enough, Lord" (1 Kings 19:4). "He has driven me away and made me walk in darkness rather than light" (Lamentations 3:2). Even Jesus in Gethsemane confesses, "My soul is overwhelmed with sorrow to the point of death." Not one is condemned. Heaven welcomes this kind of truth. God never rebukes honest lament. He does rebuke tidy answers that blame the sufferer (Job's well-meaning friends), but He never rebukes a broken heart.

Yet there is a difference between lament and bitterness. Lament says, I do not understand, but I am turning toward You. Bitterness says, you did this, and I am turning away. Naomi stands in the fragile space between both. She has just spoken God's name in blessing, which signals that she is still in a relationship with Him. The thread of her faith is thin, but it is still holding. What she cannot yet see is that God's hand has not turned against her. It is guiding her along this very road. It is preserving her "sha'ar," her remnant, even now. Divine timing is breathing around her steps, shaping the path long before she recognizes it. But Naomi cannot see any of this yet. She sees only the grave markers behind her. When loss becomes your interpreter, you miss the presence that walks beside you.

DIVINE TIMING INSIGHT

God does not need us to feel ready, whole, or perfect before he can create providence in our lives. Even though Naomi believes she is walking toward a future that has already collapsed, heaven is still aligning restoration around her grief. She thinks the Lord's hand has turned against her, when in truth it is the very hand guiding her steps back to Bethlehem, the one place where redemption has been waiting to meet her. Divine timing moves even when our faith is threadbare. It arranges provision while we speak despair, orchestrates arrivals while we assume abandonment, and guides us home long before we understand why our feet will not stop moving. Naomi cannot see it yet, but loss is not the narrator of her story; God is. And divine timing often feels like emptiness just before it becomes resurrection.

TRACING YOUR OWN THREADS OF DIVINE TIMING

"I am forgotten as though I were dead; I have become like broken pottery." (Psalm 31:12)

Where do I feel overlooked, or forgotten—and how might God be holding the pieces of my story even when I don't see him?

"Call to me, and I will answer you and tell you great and unsearchable things you do not know." (Jeremiah 33:3).

Where am I wrestling with doubt or silence, and what would it look like to bring my questions to God rather than hide them?

"You have taken from me friend and neighbor—darkness is my closest friend." (Psalm 88:18).

Do I feel surrounded by darkness, and how might God be nearer to me in the shadows than I have dared to believe?

FILL-IN REFLECTION

What pain from my past have I walked away from, not believing that light can one day shine through?

____

____

____

____

What would it look like for God to meet me in the dark places that I'm too broken to name?

____

____

____

____

____

____

Where do I feel alone in ways I've never spoken aloud? How can I let God meet me in these places?

DAY 6: RUTH 1:14-15

Again they wept aloud, and Orpah kissed her mother-in-law goodbye, but Ruth clung to her. "Look," said Naomi, "your sister-in-law has gone back to her people and her gods. Follow your sister-in-law" (BSB)

The reasonable path and the wisest path rarely point in the same direction. Sometimes they fork so sharply that you can feel the pull of both in your chest. One promises safety. The other demands faith. One protects what you have. The other risks everything for who you might become.

Still on the road from Moab, heading west toward Bethlehem, the weeping rises again. Naomi's sorrow and firmness hang over them and drive Orpah to make a choice. One last kiss to Naomi. And it is final. I love you, but I cannot follow this road, and she turns back toward the green hills of Moab. A wise, understandable, and logical choice. She did the mental math; took in the bleak arithmetic of impossibility. Scripture neither shames nor scolds her. It simply records: Orpah kisses her mother-in-law goodbye.

Orpah's name hauntingly disappears. We never hear of her again. She joins Lot's wife, who also disappears from the pages of Scripture, but the two are very different women: Lot's wife disobeyed a direct divine command and faced immediate judgment. She couldn't help but look back at Sodom even as destruction rained down behind her. The past called to her louder than God's promise of safety ahead. A backward glance cost her everything; a pillar of salt marked the spot where she chose memory over mercy, nostalgia over obedience.

Orpah's choice was different. There's no hint at judgment and no visible consequence. At this crossroad, both women are loved, but only one becomes part of the story that changes everything.

DIVINE TIMING INSIGHT

Both women loved Naomi. Both faced the same choice. But only one understood that divine timing can sometimes disguise itself as foolishness to the world. Orpah made the reasonable choice.

Ruth made the covenant choice. And history remembers only one of them.

TRACING YOUR OWN THREADS OF DIVINE TIMING

"For the foolishness of God is wiser than human wisdom, and the weakness of God is stronger than human strength." (1 Corinthians 1:25)

Have I ever found myself stepping out from a logical, worldly choice, and discovering that it was not only wise but serendipitous?

"This is what the Lord says: 'Stand at the crossroads and look; ask for the ancient paths, ask where the good way is, and walk in it, and you will find rest for your souls.'" (Jeremiah 6:16)

What if I memorized this verse and used it as a daily reminder? How would my life change?

FILL-IN REFLECTION

I'm standing at a crossroads between path 1, the reasonable choice.

____

____

____

This path offers:

____

____

____

Why does it make sense:

____

____

____

What it would cost me:

____

____

____

Path 2, the costly and uncertain choice. This path requires:

____

____

____

What I'd be leaving behind:

____

____

____

Why might it feel like foolishness?

____

____

What it might lead to if I trust God:

____

____

____

What I sense God whispering:

____

____

____

The fear that holds me back:

____

____

____

____

____

____

____

____

DAY 7: RUTH 1:16-18

But Ruth replied, "Do not urge me to leave you or to turn back from following you. For where you go, I will go, and where you stay, I will stay. Your people will be my people, and your God will be my God. Where you die, I will die, and there I will be buried. May the LORD punish me, and ever so severely, if anything but death separates you and me." When Naomi saw that Ruth was determined to go with her, she stopped trying to persuade her (BSB)

You have heard the words in these verses before, but you likely do not know that they came from the mouth of a Moabite woman standing on the wreckage of life. Spoken by a descendant of a people east of Judah, who worship Chemosh. A people whom God banned from the assembly of the Lord for ten generations. Spoken by a woman with no claim on Israel's God and no promise of a future in Naomi's land. Yet, it is she who speaks the most covenant-rich lines in all of Scripture.

Even though the words are echoed in passages and lyrics at weddings, they are not the language of romance. They are words about love, yes, but they go much deeper. They portray a loyalty so fierce that it almost defies common sense.

Ruth speaks these famous words on a dusty road, with nothing to offer and nothing to gain except the bond of a bitter, grieving widow. The timing and location matter too; she makes her vow before crossing into the promised land, before she has a chance to see what it offers.

She speaks the words with defiance; she is not pleading but speaking with a sternness and clarity that come from a heart so profound that logic cannot dislodge them. No fear can unmake it.

"Don't urge me to leave you or to turn back from you." Not a request, but a refusal. A line drawn in dust that becomes permanent. Not asking for permission but declaring intention. Don't waste a breath trying to stop me, don't release me with blessing. Don't waste your time. I am not leaving.

"Where you go, I will go, and where you stay, I will stay." Geography. Movement. Dwelling. Every step, every stopping place, every future location, bound together. No dividing of paths when circumstances get hard. Wherever Naomi's road leads, Ruth's road follows.

"Your people will be my people and your God my God." She's renouncing everything. Not just her homeland, but her identity. Not just her family, but her gods as well. Not just her past, but her future as she imagined it. In the ancient world, your people and your gods were inseparable. Ruth is saying: I am becoming an Israelite.

"Where you die, I will die, and there I will be buried." The final seal. The ultimate commitment. Not just life, but death. To be buried in foreign soil, as were Elimelek, Mahlon, and Kilion, was to be cut off, forgotten, erased from the memory of your people. Your grave was your final testimony to where you belonged, who your people were.

Ruth says, 'Even in death, I will not be separated from you. 'Even in the grave, my bones will testify that I belonged to your people, worshiped your God, walked your path. My final resting place will not be in Moab among the bones of my fathers, but in Bethlehem among the bones of yours.

"May the LORD deal with me, be it ever so severely, if even death separates you and me." And now—the oath. The binding, irrevocable vow. She's invoking Yahweh's name. Not Chemosh. Not the gods of Moab. But the God of Israel, the God she's just declared as her own, the God whose name she's speaking for perhaps the first time with this weight of commitment. Chai YHWH—as the LORD lives. It's the strongest oath an Israelite could make, calling down God's judgment if the vow is broken.

And Ruth, Ruth the Moabite, Ruth who shouldn't even know this formula, Ruth who has no standing to invoke covenant language, speaks it anyway.

May God Himself deal with me- harshly—severely, with full weight of divine judgment, if I break this vow; if I let even death separate us. She is invoking the language of Genesis 2:24, where a man holds fast to his wife. The Hebrew word is "Dabaq." To cling. To cleave. To hold fast with a strength that bends circumstance to commitment. I am rewriting my identity. I am stepping into a new story. I am becoming someone I wasn't before. And there's no going back.

The Hebrew word used to describe Ruth's sternness is "amats," to be strong, firm, resolute, obstinate in a way that can't be moved. It's the word used for courage that doesn't waver, for determination that won't be talked out of itself, for a decision so settled that no argument could unseat it.

And Naomi, finally, sees it. Ruth's declaration is not a fleeting impulse or a passing, trivial emotion. Done, already sealed, beyond reversal.

Something has been rising in Ruth during this walk beside Naomi, and now we see it: A recognition. A hunger. A knowing that the God of Israel is nothing like Chemosh. Chemosh demands sacrifice. Yahweh restores. Chemosh devours. Yahweh pursues. Ruth senses it in Naomi's stubborn faith.

So, now two women, two widows, walk. One Hebrew returning, one Moabite leaving. One bitter, one determined. One convinced God has abandoned her, one stepping toward a God she's only beginning to know. Mile after mile, they walk the fifty-mile road from Moab to Bethlehem. Through rocky terrain, past landmarks Ruth has never seen, closer with each step to a future that exists only in faith and the stubborn conviction that where Naomi goes, God goes too; and that's reason enough to follow.

DIVINE TIMING INSIGHT

Paul will later write that the "foolishness of God is wiser than human wisdom and the weakness of God is stronger than human strength" (1 Corinthians 1:25). Ruth stands there, proof of it. Her choice looks foolish. Reckless. Impossible to justify. Yet somehow wiser than every reasonable calculation, Orpah makes. Jeremiah writes that the Lord invites us to stand at the crossroads and look; to ask for the ancient paths and walk in them so we may find rest for our souls (Jeremiah 6:16). Ruth seems to understand this without hearing the words. She chooses the ancient path instead of the easy one. She chooses becoming over belonging. Purpose over safety. God over certainty.

TRACING YOUR OWN THREADS OF DIVINE TIMING

"There is a friend who sticks closer than a brother." (Proverbs 18:24)
> What keeps me from being a loyal friend—fear, busyness, self-protection?

"Let love and faithfulness never leave you… then you will win favor." (Proverbs 3:3–4)
> How can I embody both hesed (faithful love) and emet (truth) in the relationships God has entrusted to me?

"For I desire steadfast love (hesed) and not sacrifice." (Hosea 6:6)
> Where have I offered God performance instead of presence?

FILL-IN REFLECTION

If I rewrote Ruth's vow in my own words, it would sound like:
Do not urge me to:

____

____

____

I will go with:

____

____

____

I will stay where:

____

____

____

Will be my:

____

____

____

____

____

____

____

____

May the Lord deal with me severely if I

____

____

____

The fear I must release to commit:

____

____

____

The faith I must embrace:

____

____

____

What would determination, "amats," look like for me?

DAY 8: RUTH 1:19-21

So Naomi and Ruth traveled on until they came to Bethlehem. And when they arrived, the whole town was stirred because of them, and the women exclaimed, "Can this be Naomi?" "Do not call me Naomi," she answered. "Call me Mara, because the Almighty has dealt very bitterly with me. I went away full, but the LORD has brought me back empty. Why call me Naomi? The LORD has testified against me, and the Almighty has brought calamity upon me" (BSB)

They've been walking for days now, across rocky ground that twists ankles, and streams that, after the drought, finally remember what it's like to flow with water again. The land shifts from Moabite to Hebrew, from unfamiliar to familiar, from exile to a home that feels almost like a mirage.

Naomi's arrival stirred the town. The Hebrew word is "hum." It means to be stirred up, troubled, in turmoil; shaken from complacency into a state of reaction. (Ruth 1:19). Small-town surprise woven with uncertainty. Whispers ripple through the gate like wind through wheat. "Can this be Naomi?" (Ruth 1:19). Not a question of identity, but a question of semblance. The Hebrew is Ha zot Naomi. Can this woman, hollowed by grief, be Naomi? Naomi, the Pleasant one? The Naomi who left full?

The last time Naomi walked this land, Elimelek, Mahlon, and Kilion were by her side; just for a short stay, until the rains returned, just until the drought was over. Just until life calmed down, now, she returns alone, with no husband or sons. Only Ruth is by her side, a Moabite woman who brings a complication. Ruth's presence marks them as outsiders, her accent, her walk, her heritage; all of it is a reminder of their foreignness.

Naomi wears grief like a second skin. After fifty miles of walking, her clothes hang loose, her eyes are dim, and her silhouette speaks of loss. The townspeople don't recognize her. They see only the weight of her sorrow, the signs of hardship that have reshaped her.

When she names herself Mara, bitter, from Naomi, pleasant, there is something courageous in the way she names it, something fastidious and true. (Ruth 1:20). However, notice this detail: in her complaint, she is still referring to God and invoking His name;

still wrestling, not denying that He's there. She embodies what the psalmist echoes when he says that the Lord is close to the brokenhearted and saves those who are crushed in spirit (Psalm 34:18).

God isn't offended by her honesty. Her lament doesn't threaten Him. Naomi's naming isn't just the truth—it's the start of something new. You can't heal from what you refuse to name. Naomi calls God by two names: Yahweh, the covenant God, and Shaddai, the Almighty, the One who has the power to shape history. This wrestling, even in her sorrow, shows there's still a relationship; strained, but real. You can't change what you won't name. So, she names it. "I am Mara. I am bitter. Stop calling me pleasant."

DIVINE TIMING INSIGHT

Naomi returns to Bethlehem empty, bitter, and convinced God has afflicted her. But here's what God's timing reveals: Naomi's theology is wrong. But she is back in the covenant land. She's returned to the place where redemption can find her. Sometimes, God allows us to arrive in the right place with the wrong interpretation, trusting that proximity to His purposes will eventually correct our perspective.

TRACING YOUR OWN THREADS OF DIVINE TIMING

"The Lord builds up Jerusalem; he gathers the exiles of Israel. He heals the brokenhearted and binds up their wounds." (Psalm 147:2-3)

Are there places where I feel scattered—emotionally, spiritually, or relationally? How might God be gathering me back to wholeness one piece at a time?

"My eyes fail from weeping, I am in torment within; my heart is poured out on the ground because my people are destroyed, because children and infants faint in the streets of the city. My soul refuses to be comforted." (Lamentations 2:11)

Bookmark this entry. Save it for a day when you need God to remind you of his promises and make this your prayer.

FILL-IN REFLECTION

A part of my heart that still feels exiled or far from home:

____

____

____

A wound I keep covered:

____

____

____

A place where I have resisted comfort because pain feels safer than hope:

____

____

____

____

____

____

____

____

DAY 9: RUTH 1:22

So Naomi returned from the land of Moab with her daughter-in-law Ruth the Moabitess. And they arrived in Bethlehem at the beginning of the barley harvest (BSB)

A short note at the end of the verse. Blink, and you might miss it. *"They arrived in Bethlehem just as the barley harvest was beginning"* (Ruth 1:22). Too soon, and the fields would still be bare. Too late, and the gleaning would already be gone. But they arrive precisely when food is available for those who have nothing. The words are easy to skim over, yet shimmering with providence: They arrive just as the barley harvest begins. God's timing is already moving toward them long before either woman feels even the faintest pulse of it.

Provision is already rising around them, ripening in the very moment they arrive, prepared long before either woman knew she would ever need it. Ancient law and present need lock into place with perfect precision. God not only wrote the law that provides for the poor and vulnerable to glean the barley fields for food, but He also timed their arrival for such a time as this. Two women, empty and grieving, enter the town with no plan at all, yet walk straight into divine timing so exact it mimics coincidence. Two women cross the threshold of Bethlehem during the single season when a poor foreign woman can gather grain and survive. And not just any season, but the season when Israel remembers that death passes over homes marked by blood, the season when the first fruits are waved before God as a sign of what is coming. Redemption season. Restoration season. The season of beginnings. Ruth arrives as the barley harvest is beginning because redemption is also just beginning.

This is how Paul will one day describe this unfolding: God marks out appointed geographical boundaries and seasons so people might seek Him (Acts 17:26-27), and that His plan unfolds when the times reach their fulfillment (Ephesians 1:9-10). Scripture bursts with stories like this:

Insomnia causes a king to read the royal chronicles, where the scroll just happens to fall open to Mordecai's forgotten loyalty. (Esther 6:1–3).

Rebekah steps out to draw water the very minute Abraham's servant finishes praying. (Genesis 24:12–15).

A boy walks past the right doorway, catching whispered plans and carrying the warning that saves Paul's life into Roman corridors. (Acts 23:16–22).

Provision is never improvisational. God still positions people for good. He still aligns steps so that when you finally arrive, exhausted and empty, you discover that provision has been waiting for you. Naomi feels late; too late for her life to be restored. But she is arriving at the beginning. She feels empty. But emptiness frees her to receive.

DIVINE TIMING INSIGHT

The barley harvest is the first harvest, appointed by law for widows and foreigners. Too soon, and the fields would be bare. Too late, and the gleaning would be gone. However, Ruth and Naomi arrive just as the provisions are ready, and the law makes space for the vulnerable.

TRACING YOUR OWN THREADS OF DIVINE TIMING

"Wait for the Lord; be strong and take heart and wait for the Lord."
(Psalm 27:14)

> Where is God asking me to hold my ground with courage rather than rush ahead in fear, trusting that strength is born in the waiting?

"But those who hope in the LORD will renew their strength. They will soar on wings like eagles; they will run and not grow weary, will walk and not be faint." (Isaiah 40:31)

> How could I begin to find the rest and strength that God provides?

"Be still before the Lord and wait patiently for him." (Psalm 37:7)

What part of my life is God inviting me to unclench and release—choosing stillness over striving, patience over panic?

FILL-IN REFLECTION

A place where God is asking me to take heart instead of taking control:

____

____

____

A part of my life where I am weary and in need of God's renewal:

____

____

____

A situation where God is inviting me to be still instead of striving:

____

____

____

____

____

DAY 10: RUTH 2:1-3

Now Naomi had a relative on her husband's side, a man of standing from the clan of Elimelech, whose name was Boaz. And Ruth the Moabitess said to Naomi, "Please let me go to the field and glean heads of grain after someone in whose sight I may find favor." "Go ahead, my daughter," she replied. So she went out and entered a field and began to glean behind the harvesters. And as it turned out, she was working in a field belonging to Boaz, who was from the clan of Elimelech (BSB)

Starvation is certain if Ruth does not go out and find food. Ruth rises with the dawn and turns her steps toward the fields. Because of the vow Ruth made, to bind herself to Israel's God (Ruth 1:16-17), Ruth is a "ger," and so she walks not as a beggar, but as one claimed by the law itself.

God has intentionally created laws (Leviticus 19:9-10, 23:22; Deuteronomy 24:19-22) to protect the vulnerable. "The stranger, the fatherless, and the widow," the ancient words declare, and Ruth wears all these mantles: "ger" and widow both, wrapped in divine provision. She does not come pleading for scraps of mercy or casting herself upon landowners' whims. The God she has chosen has already spoken her name in the margins of the harvest law. The corners of the fields, the fallen grain, the overlooked sheaves: these are hers by right, left there by heaven's command. Still, she moves through a world that may not see what God has written, where threat and scorn wait in the furrows as surely as barley.

Even though she is protected by law, there are still risks (Ruth 2:9). So she works in the margins, vulnerable to harassment, assault, or being driven from the fields entirely. She keeps herself bent low, as if the back-breaking work weren't burden enough, hoping to gather what she needs without incident. But today, despite every careful step, she will be discovered.

"...As it turned out, she is working in the field belonging to Boaz" (Ruth 2:3).

Here, the writer of the Book of Ruth is sending us a divine wink, disguised as a grammatical stumble. Done intentionally to draw our attention to the irony. A joke from this ancient writer. The phrase in question is, "as it turned out." It is one we will read again in this story. The Hebrew word is "miqreh." Chance. Accident. Happenstance. Except, here, the Hebrew writer repeats the word, so that the text literally says, "her chance chanced upon Boaz's field." to us: The writer is saying, 'Can you believe it?' Of all the fields Ruth could pick, she chose this one. Owned by Boaz. Providence dressed as coincidence. God is hiding in plain sight, orchestrating all the events that unfold. This doubled phrasing isn't common; it appears in 1 Samuel 6:9, when the Philistines are trying to figure out whether their recent string of bad luck might be due to the Ark of the Covenant, which they had stolen. We will see this little joke reappear in Ruth 4.

As it turns out, Naomi's dead husband, Elimelek, does still have a relative living in Bethlehem. He's the one who stayed behind during the famine on Day 1 of this devotional. So far, in this story, he's been waiting behind the curtain, but you can be sure that God is very present in his life. Now, the curtain begins to lift on him.

Ruth had no map of the local landowners; she didn't meet with the town's women to find out who the most eligible bachelors were or where to find them. She simply showed up for work. In the best possible field she could find, as it turned out. God's gentle whisper: that our steps are established by the LORD (Psalm 37:23).

DIVINE TIMING INSIGHT

Part of what makes Bible stories so endearing is the perfect timing that appears and eases the tension in ways the human mind never could have predicted. From Joseph to Moses, to David, you see the story of God's providence, disguised as ordinary decisions. Providence is wearing the clothes of chance. Orchestration so subtle that it appears to be luck.

TRACING YOUR OWN THREADS OF DIVINE TIMING

"The Lord directs the steps of the righteous." (Psalm 37:23)

How could ordinary responsibilities—small, unglamorous routines be placing me exactly where God intends to meet me?

"In their hearts humans plan their course, but the Lord establishes their steps." (Proverbs 16:9)

What random events from your life have ended up being the best thing that could have happened: Events you could not have planned even if you tried?

"And my God will meet all your needs according to the riches of His glory." (Philippians 4:19)

Where do I need to let go and start trusting that God is already making a way, even before I recognize the need?

FILL-IN REFLECTION

A time when I "just happened" to be in the right place at the right time:

____

____

____

____

A person who "just happened" to cross my path when I needed them:

____

____

____

____

An opportunity that "just happened" to open up?

____

____

____

____

Looking back, I can see God's hand in it because:

____

____

____

____

____

____

____

____

____

____

____

____

____

____

____

____

DAY 11: RUTH2:4-9

Just then Boaz arrived from Bethlehem and said to the harvesters, "The LORD be with you." "The LORD bless you," they replied. Boaz asked the foreman of his harvesters, "Whose young woman is this?" The foreman answered, "She is the Moabite who returned with Naomi from the land of Moab. She asked, 'Please let me glean and gather among the sheaves after the harvesters.' She has been on her feet since morning until now, except for a short rest in the shelter." Then Boaz said to Ruth, "Listen, my daughter. Do not go and glean in another field, and do not go away from here. Stay here with my servant girls. Let your eyes be on the field they are harvesting, and follow along after them. I have ordered the young men not to touch you. And when you are thirsty, go and drink from the jars the young men have filled" (BSB).

Two small words that slip past in the text if you read them too quickly: Just then. Just then, Boaz arrives from Bethlehem. Not an hour earlier. Not after Ruth has gone home. Just then, while she bends low in the barley, trying to remain unnoticed. She is unaware that the one man who can change the trajectory of her life is walking toward her.

The boss arrives. Instead of hiding from the man who holds authority, the workers receive a blessing from Boaz and offer him the same.

The air is thick with chaff floating like pale gold snow, sickles swinging, sheaves thudding, as the workers wipe sweat from their brows with their forearms. In the middle of ordered chaos, workers, foremen, gleaners from all walks of life, Boaz still manages to recognize Ruth among so many. The woman with the dust of Moab still on her sandals, now mixing with Bethlehem soil. His instincts give us a glimpse of the way the true Shepherd sees His own, the way He calls them by name before anyone else does (John 10:3).

His question about Ruth tells the whole truth about the world she lives in: "Who does that young woman belong to?" Not who is she? Whose is she? Because in this land, belonging is protection. And she belongs to no one. This first question about her, Who does she belong to?" will hang in the air for the rest of the story. Later, on the threshing floor under a canopy of stars, he will ask another question about who she is; and her identity and her sense of belonging will have transformed.

Boaz hears more than the words spoken in the answers; he gathers the entire picture of her; he discerns her work ethic, her loyalty and honor to Naomi, and the honor she brings to her dead husband.

When he gives her access to his water, this echoes an ancient gesture that says, "You are welcome here." Ancient wells served as meeting places, signposts of belonging, and symbols of new beginnings. Abraham and Abimelech's treaty, Isaac's servants digging new beginnings, Jacob first seeing Rachel, and rolling away the stone.

DIVINE TIMING INSIGHT

Boaz arriving "just then" is not a coincidence; it's God's choreography. Boaz arrives at the exact moment Ruth is bent low in the barley, unseen by the world but fully seen by God. If he had come earlier, he would have missed her. If she had arrived later, she would have slipped through the cracks of anonymity. But the God who governs harvest cycles and human hearts aligns their steps on the same patch of earth at the same breath of time. Divine timing threads people into our story, not a moment too soon and never a moment too late. It places us in the right field, under the right sun, in front of the right eyes—long before we understand the significance of where we're standing.

TRACING YOUR OWN THREADS OF DIVINE TIMING

"My times are in your hands." (Psalm 31:15)
>Where am I anxious about timing, fearing I'm too late or too early? What would it look like to trust that God is not rushed, not delayed, and never imprecise with my life?

"Your ears will hear a voice behind you, saying, 'This is the way; walk in it.'" (Isaiah 30:21)
>Where is God whispering guidance in the middle of what feels chaotic or mundane? How might He be directing me even when I can't yet see the outcome of my obedience?

"Before they call, I will answer; while they are still speaking, I will hear." (Isaiah 65:24)

Where have I seen God answer something before I even knew to ask for it—my own *just then* moments? What provision might God already be moving toward me that I have not yet noticed?

FILL-IN REFLECTION

A time when someone saw me, really saw me, and it changed something:

____

____

____

The hard work I'm doing right now that feels unseen:

____

____

____

A way I can show that kindness to someone else:

____

____

____

____

____

DAY 12: RUTH 2:10-13

At this, she fell on her face, bowing to the ground, and said to him, "Why have I found favor in your eyes that you should take notice of me, although I am a foreigner?" Boaz replied, "I have been told all about what you have done for your mother-in-law since the death of your husband, how you left your father and mother and your land of birth and came to live with a people you did not know before. May the LORD repay you for your deeds. May you receive a full reward from the LORD, the God of Israel, under whose wings you have taken refuge." "My lord," she said, "I have found favor in your sight, for you have comforted and spoken kindly to your servant, though I am not like one of your maidservants" (BSB)

Notice that what moves Ruth to joyfulness in the barley field is not the extra gain she receives, but the words that Boaz speaks over her: While the reflection Ruth sees in the water is that of a lowly Moabite, scavenging in the dust for a day's meal, Boaz names what she thought no one noticed.

Boaz knows that the ache of an empty stomach can't be satiated with food alone. But the hunger of the soul doesn't live in the body, and Ruth carries that kind of hunger. Ruth has made choices that required sacrifice. Each one had better alternatives that would have been better for her, but not for Naomi. Those choices have made it harder for Ruth to walk her road. Boaz's recognition and honor of them feeds Ruth's soul more than grain ever could. The choices made in the dark that cost everything. The faithfulness that had no witnesses.

In a culture where Moabites were historically excluded (Deuteronomy 23:3), Boaz offers her refuge and covenant language without hesitation. He doesn't hint at treating her foreignness as a flaw and extends to her a place under the wings of the God of Israel. The phrase "under his wings," Hebrew "tachat kenafav," is ancient covenant language from Psalm 91:4. Jesus will echo this same tenderness when He says He longs to gather His people as a hen gathers her chicks. (Matthew 23:37). Boaz does not see her as a Moabite scavenging in the dust, not as a foreign widow with no way into the covenant community. Instead, he sees someone who has been faithful to others since her husband's death.

She asks him, "Why have I found such favor in your eyes that you notice a foreigner?" The word she uses is "nokriyyah," foreigner, outsider, the one who doesn't belong. She still names herself by her displacement. She still carries the label of an outsider. But Boaz names what she cannot yet claim: courage, faith, belonging.

Ruth arrives to gather grain for the pantry, and she leaves this field with language that begins to restore her identity. Boaz speaks life over Ruth before he gives her bread. He restores her identity before feeding her. Words come first. Provision follows. He names her future before she can see it forming.

DIVINE TIMING INSIGHT

Wholeness is not always restored through grand gestures, dramatic moments, or public declarations. God inspires and directs us to deliver just the right words at just the right moment to rebuild what sorrow dismantled. Words heal; He knows that words alone can restore identity and dignity. Words arriving, just before someone needs to hear them.

TRACING YOUR OWN THREADS OF DIVINE TIMING

"He will cover you with his feathers, and under his wings you will find refuge; his faithfulness will be your shield and rampart." (Psalm 91:4)

What if the space I need to let go is already part of my life? Am I so focused on what I lack that I'm overlooking the ease God is already giving me?

"Gracious words are a honeycomb, sweet to the soul and healing to the bones." (Proverbs 16:24)

Is there someone who needs me to encourage them? How could I be part of the sweetness that lifts their Spirit?

"Therefore, encourage one another and build each other up, just as in fact you are doing." (1 Thessalonians 5:11)

Who are people that God has placed in my path for now, not later, that I can intentionally build up and encourage?

FILL-IN REFLECTION

I feel God telling me to rest in this area of my life:

____

____

____

God is inviting me now to encourage:

____

____

____

Words I can speak are:

____

____

____

____

____

____

____

____

____

DAY 13: RUTH 2:14-16

At this, she fell on her face, bowing to the ground, and said to him, "Why have I found favor in your eyes that you should take notice of me, although I am a foreigner?" Boaz replied, "I have been told all about what you have done for your mother-in-law since the death of your husband, how you left your father and mother and your land of birth and came to live with a people you did not know before. May the LORD repay you for your deeds. May you receive a full reward from the LORD, the God of Israel, under whose wings you have taken refuge." "My lord," she said, "I have found favor in your sight, for you have comforted and spoken kindly to your servant, though I am not like one of your maidservants" (BSB)

Warm, toasted kernels placed in her palm. Bread shared on a hot day in the middle of a barley field. And then the "chometz" (sour wine) thinned with water, sharp on the tongue, restoring what the sun had stolen. This elixir was the ancient laborer's version of today's energy drinks that athletes reach for, which started as a yellowish-green pickle brine—salty and briny, stirring strength to rise again by replenishing what the sun steals.

Centuries later, during this same harvest season of Passover, a small boy will offer the scraps in a basket: five barley loaves and two fish. Not nearly enough. And Jesus will bless it so that it feeds five thousand (John 6:1-13). A miracle that rejects scarcity's lie.

Boaz asks the workers to pull out stalks from their bundles and leave them behind for Ruth. Grain meant for the wealthy owners is scattered like small mercies at her feet. Boaz keeps the law, then gives more, proving that the law creates a floor, not a ceiling, for grace. He embodies hesed, covenant love that overflows.

Ruth, the Moabite, is invited to sit at the table of an Israelite landowner. A radical disruption of protocol. She is fed until she is satisfied, then rises to gather more. Provision spills over, abundance measured not only in the weight of grain but in the invitation to stay, to return, to belong.

In this story, in this barley field, the hungry are satisfied, the stranger is welcomed, the outsider is folded into covenant belonging.

DIVINE TIMING INSIGHT

Everything in this scene pivots on grace and timing; Ruth arrives at the very start of barley harvest, stepping into Boaz's field. Even the chometz shared at midday ties her to the season of Passover, a feast that remembers the God who feeds His people when they have nothing left. These alignments aren't loose coincidences; they are the undercurrent of divine timing, where ordinary moments become turning points and provisions arrive exactly when the heart is sure they won't. But sometimes, so focused on events, we fail to see the hand orchestrating everything behind the scenes, ensuring that we are folded into His divine plan.

TRACING YOUR OWN THREADS OF DIVINE TIMING

"The steps of a good man are ordered by the Lord." (Psalms 37:23)
How often do I decide first, then pray after? What if I inverted that—brought God the question before I decide?

"The plans of the diligent lead to profit as surely as haste leads to poverty." (Proverbs 21:5)
What "quick fixes" have I been choosing—and what fruit have they produced?

"At the proper time we will reap a harvest if we do not give up." (Galatians 6:9)
There is a fine line between surrender and giving up. Am I releasing control to God, or am I just quitting?

FILL-IN REFLECTION

I sense God is ordering my steps in:

____

____

____

____

I need to surrender and release into God's hands:

____

____

I am asking for endurance in:

____

____

____

____

____

____

____

____

____

____

____

____

DAY 14: RUTH 2:17-23

So Ruth gleaned in the field until evening. Then she beat out what she had gleaned, and it was about an ephah of barley. She picked it up and went into the town, where her mother-in-law saw what she had gleaned. Ruth also brought out and gave her what she had left over after she was satisfied. Her mother-in-law asked her, "Where did you glean today, and where did you work? Blessed be the man who noticed you." Then Ruth told her mother-in-law about the man with whom she had worked. "The name of the man I worked with today is Boaz," she said. "May he be blessed by the LORD, who has not withdrawn His kindness from the living or the dead." Naomi continued, "The man is our close relative; he is one of our kinsman-redeemers." Then Ruth the Moabitess said, "He also told me, 'Stay with my young men until they have finished harvesting all my grain.'" And Naomi said to her daughter-in-law Ruth, "It is good, my daughter, for you to go out with his servant girls, so that nothing will happen to you in another field." So Ruth stayed close to the servant girls of Boaz to glean until the barley and wheat harvests were finished. And she lived with her mother-in-law (BSB)

Hope does not always arrive with thunder, fireworks, and sunshine and roses. More often, it comes in tiny parcels like this: In an ordinary moment, when a girl comes home from work and drops a simple bundle of grain and the remnants of a leftover meal on the table.

When Ruth measures her day's work, she has about an ephah of barley, nearly thirty pounds, enough grain to sustain two women for over a week. Far more than any gleaner should gather. Abundance.

Naomi sees the weight of it, the evidence of labor and kindness mingled together with the grace that Ruth says the man showed her in the field. Ruth reaches into her garment and draws out the leftovers from her own meal, bread broken earlier now offered whole in the giving, a second abundance. Naomi is astonished and asks questions that will pivot this story and God's work toward redemption. Where did you glean today? Where did you work?

"The name of the man I worked with today is Boaz." With a single name spoken, Naomi's entire world shifts, and she begins to see her world much differently. Now, with the clarity of Jacob waking from his sleep with a stone beneath his head, who whispered, Surely the Lord is in this place, and I was not aware of it (Genesis 28), a fresh, sweet recognition overcomes Naomi; God has been building a ladder between her grief and His purpose, just for her.

Naomi begins speaking blessings in a way she has not heard herself say in years. "The LORD bless him. He has not stopped showing his kindness to the living and the dead" (Ruth 2:20). Like the disciples on the road to Emmaus, who later realized their hearts had been burning as they walked with the stranger before they knew who He was (Luke 24:13-32). God has been walking with her, too, all this time, hidden, until now; until gleaning became grace, until survival became blessing, until a meal was offered by a man named Boaz.

The scattered fragments of Naomi's story come together in alignment. The famine that once crushed her now appears redeemed for good. The earlier whisper of rain, the faint scent of petrichor drifting into Moab as news reached her ears, now reveals itself as a signal of change. Ruth gleaning in Boaz's field is no accident.

Naomi has not thought about the go'el in years. Loss has buried the thought. Husband gone. Sons gone. Identity unraveling. Future erased. Too bitter to imagine restoration. Too empty to hope. But now, with thirty pounds of barley dropped before her and Boaz's name echoing in her mind, she remembers the law God wrote to protect women like her. She awakens to the possibility. Her thoughts gather themselves into a pattern. She sees the outline of a plan forming.

Boaz is a relative. A kinsman redeemer. The possibility she had buried beneath her grief now stands in front of her with a name—the "go'el" (kinsman redeemer) she did not dare to dream of. The Spirit of truth brings clarity, and her thoughts begin to coalesce into a plan. She does not have all the answers yet; she will still need God's providence to intervene in events so that the plan can unfold.

The plan she's building has just enough fragility that it risks falling apart entirely. She doesn't know how this can all work, or even if it can; there is so much risk. For one, Ruth is a Moabite; Boaz is an Israelite. Her standing as a ger had opened the fields to her, given her the right to glean. But the scroll still names her 'Ruth the Moabite' (Ruth 2:6, 21; 4:5, 10), and Deuteronomy's words echo in her memory: no Moabite may enter the assembly of the LORD (23:3). Would the elders approve of this marriage? Would the community accept it?

But it is not in the facts that faith is built; it is through hopelessness and uncertainty that we learn to trust Him. This is precisely how faith is built, not in certainty. As Abraham learned on Mount Moriah in Genesis 22, faith is built when the way looks impossible.

DIVINE TIMING INSIGHT

"Hope deferred makes the heart sick, but a longing fulfilled is a tree of life" (Proverbs 13:12). Naomi has lived ten years with deferred hope. But a longing fulfilled is a tree of life. All it took was thirty pounds of barley at her feet and the sound of Boaz's name in her ears to see that God was there all along. Hope doesn't return through a miracle. It returns through recognition. Divine timing gives you just enough pieces at just the right moment until the picture finally forms.

TRACING YOUR OWN THREADS OF DIVINE TIMING

"You, O Lord, are a God merciful and gracious, slow to anger and abounding in loyal love." "Blessed are those who have not seen and yet have believed." (John 20:29)

> Am I waiting for proof when God is asking me to step out in faith? Is God building my faith through a season of waiting?

"Surely the Lord is in this place, and I was not aware of it." Genesis 28:16

> What am I missing today? Where am I taking for granted the ways that God shows up for me?

"For I know the plans I have for you, plans to give you hope and a future." Jeremiah 29:11

> How would I approach my days as if I really believed this?

FILL-IN REFLECTION

Something in my life that once felt like a loss but may have been a provision:

____

____

____

Think of a person, a circumstance, or even a message that could be God whispering hope to you:

____

____

____

The place where I am beginning to feel life returning:

____

____

____

____

____

____

The step I sense God inviting me to take next:

____

____

____

DAY 15: RUTH 3:1-5

Then Naomi her mother-in-law said to her, "My daughter, should I not find you a resting place, that it may be well with you? Now is not Boaz our relative, with whose servant girls you have been working? Tonight he will be winnowing barley on the threshing floor. Therefore wash yourself, put on perfume, and wear your best clothes. Then go down to the threshing floor, but do not let the man know you are there until he has finished eating and drinking. When he lies down, note the place where he is lying. Then go and uncover his feet and lie down, and he will explain to you what you should do." "I will do everything you say," Ruth answered (BSB)

Hope does strange work in the hours before dawn. It moves through the mind the way a millstone moves through grain—slow, steady, grinding old thoughts into something usable, stirring what has slept for years back into motion. The thirty pounds of barley resting on the table breathe a new message into Naomi's home, filling the air with the scent of harvest, sunlight, and possibility. The warm fragrance of toasted grain slips into her spirit like yeast working through dough, lifting the 'bitter' Mara into her origins—'pleasant' Naomi—one careful rise at a time.

Rest. "Menuchah." Naomi wants this for Ruth. Not the shallow rest that comes from a full day's labor or a borrowed bed in someone else's field, but rest that settles deep into the bones, the kind that signals a future has finally taken shape. Belonging that endures beyond the next crisis. A home shaped by protection rather than surviving on the edge of a field of someone else's mercy. So, Naomi offers Ruth a plan that is both practical and daring.

She remembers the go'el, the kinsman-redeemer law from Leviticus 25. When a family fell into poverty and had to sell their land, a near relative—a go'el—had the right to buy it back, keeping the inheritance within the family line. The land could be redeemed. Elimelek's field—whether already sold or about to be sold in their desperation—could be reclaimed by a kinsman willing to pay the price.

She also remembers the levirate marriage law from Deuteronomy 25. When a man died childless, his brother was to marry the widow and raise children in the dead man's name, preserving his legacy and protecting the woman from destitution.

Two separate laws. Two different purposes.

The go'el law protects property—land, inheritance, family legacy.

The levirate law protects people—widows, children, and family lines.

But Naomi's situation requires both. She needs land redeemed and a widow protected. She needs Elimelek's inheritance restored and Ruth's future secured. The problem is that neither law was designed to work together. The go'el is not required to marry; The levirate brother is not required to redeem land.

And yet... what if they could be combined?

What makes Naomi's plan so remarkable is that what she proposes is a creative, grace-filled combination of these two separate laws—the property-redemption of the go'el, merged with the widow-protection principle of levirate marriage. No legal precedent requires this. No statute commands it. What Naomi and Ruth are about to try goes beyond the letter of the law into the heart of covenant love.

Her first obstacle is that while the law does require a kinsman redeemer to buy back family land (Leviticus 25:25), the requirement does not extend to foreign widows. Even though Ruth has captured Boaz's attention, a foreign widow does not slip easily into Israel's stories.

This entire plan she's working on could collapse at multiple points. But Naomi is a woman with no legal standing and no options. With no legal door open, Ruth is using the only remaining hope they have left with this outrageous plan that will risk everything. But even Jesus broke through unexpected channels, not the halls of power.

Daylight has already shown who Boaz is: a trustworthy, kind, generous protector; Naomi can only trust that at midnight, in the dark, Boaz will display the same character; otherwise, she could be placing Ruth in precarious danger.

Naomi deliberately works the threshing floor into her plan. An open, windy circle where wind does what hands cannot; where grain is tossed high so the chaff blows away, and the kernels fall heavy back to earth. A place where truth settles the same way the grain will; plainly, without disguise.

Boaz will be there tonight. Working, eating, settling into sleep under the open sky. Naomi works in Ezekiel's image of God laying His garment over His people as a pledge of faithfulness. (Ezekiel 16). Patterns. Threads repeating. God often works that way.

Ruth has already crossed an impossible threshold, leaving Moab with no guarantees into a world where she will be treated as an outsider. So, when Naomi presents the carefully laid-out plan to Ruth, she answers with four Hebrew words: "kol asher tomri elai ese." All that you say to me, I will do. With this affirmation, she joins the lineage of courageous biblical characters, each called out in Scripture to do something resolute, almost audacious: Rebekah, 'I will go.' Samuel, "speak, LORD, for your servant is listening." Mary, before the angel, said, "Let it be to me according to your word." In each case, none had full clarity in advance of what was required. Yet, each one, by saying yes, stepped into a story larger than themselves.

Ruth and Naomi certainly don't even know if this will be a safe mission. Ruth moves with that same steady conviction. No guarantee. No certainty. Only hesed is embodied in the willingness to take the next obedient step into the unknown. Moving into darkness, trusting that God tends to those who enter threshing floors with bold hearts. Naomi has set the plan. Ruth rises to meet it. And God is already preparing the next scene.

DIVINE TIMING INSIGHT

Sometimes we see God's laws as restrictive, and following them can feel legalistic. Yet, Scripture calls God's precepts "radiant." His boundaries, "pleasant places," and His laws are a way to walk in freedom and light. In Ruth's story, we see the opposite: the very laws that could have excluded her are the ones that Naomi uses to create a path to belonging, security, and redemption.

TRACING YOUR OWN THREADS OF DIVINE TIMING

"The boundary lines have fallen for me in pleasant places; surely I have a delightful inheritance." (Psalm 16:6)

Where could God be redrawing my boundary lines, not to restrict me, but to guide me into a place of protection, provision, or promise? Where has obedience unexpectedly brought freedom, safety, or relief?

"The Lord is good, a refuge in times of trouble. He cares for those who trust in him." (Nahum 1:7)

Am I bracing for disappointment rather than protection, or even a happy surprise? Is my default response disappointment? How can I walk in hope rather than anxiety?

FILL-IN REFLECTION

A place in my life where possibility is beginning to rise again:

____

____

____

____

A step God may be asking me to prepare for, even if I do not see the whole picture:

____

____

____

____

How do I sense that God is separating within me, the way chaff separates from grain:

____

____

____

Where I need the courage of Ruth to say, "I will do all that you ask":

DAY 16: RUTH 3:6-11

So she went down to the threshing floor and did everything her mother-in-law had instructed her to do. After Boaz had finished eating and drinking and was in good spirits, he went to lie down at the end of the grain pile. Then Ruth came secretly, uncovered his feet, and lay down. At midnight, Boaz was startled, turned over, and there was a woman lying at his feet. "Who are you?" he asked. "I am your servant Ruth," she replied. "Spread the corner of your garment over me, for you are a kinsman-redeemer." Then Boaz said, "May you be blessed by the LORD, my daughter. You have shown more kindness now than before, because you have not run after the younger men, whether rich or poor. And now do not be afraid, my daughter. I will do for you all that you request, since all my fellow townspeople know that you are a woman of noble character" (BSB)

It's good to remember, at this point in the story, in the face of Naomi's radical Old Testament plan, that the Pharisees were often shocked by Jesus—he ate with sinners, touched lepers, healed on the Sabbath, and allowed a "sinful woman" to anoint His feet. Jesus didn't conform to the "proper channels" that keep everyone in their place. Jesus was:

Born to an unwed mother (scandalous)

In a stable (improper)

Announced to shepherds (socially marginal)

Included Gentiles, tax collectors, and prostitutes (breaking boundaries)

In this story, God's redemption also breaks through the proper channels to make this rescue. Ruth and Naomi are two women on the margins, forced to risk everything because those proper channels couldn't meet their need to survive.

Naomi's plan is carefully and creatively built because it requires mutual vulnerability between Ruth, who risks her safety, reputation, and future, and Boaz, who risks his standing and integrity. Ruth goes to the threshold, the edge, the uncomfortable place where propriety and desperation meet. Redemption happens, not in the comfortable center of religious respectability, but at the risky edges.

Wrapped not only in her best garments but also cloaked in obedience and courage. The dress and the perfume are not meant to disguise Ruth but are signals that she is stepping out of widowhood's shadow. Ruth moves with deliberate steps, following Naomi's instructions to the letter.

They are specific, precise, and unnerving even to imagine. She does not know how any of this could unfold; she only knows the next faithful step to take. And tonight, on the threshing floor, a kind of sacred liturgy, preserved through famine and faith, will unfold.

From a distance, she watches Boaz. And Ruth waits. Shadowed. Steady. Suspended in the tension between command and fear. The Hebrew words here emphasize stealth rather than deception. Careful approach. Respectful distance becomes intentional nearness.

She uncovers his feet. The word is "margelot," not regel (foot), but specifically "the place at the feet," a location, a position. The narrator draws a careful boundary; the space at his feet, and lies down there, not beside him, not against him, but at the foot of him, the place where a servant would position herself before a master, where a petitioner would wait before a judge, where a covenant might be requested but cannot be presumed.

Vulnerability becomes courage. Not seduction. The willingness to be seen in need and not retreat. To risk misunderstanding, dismissal, even harm, and still choose obedience because the covenant is worth the risk.

In the field, under daylight, surrounded by witnesses, the question he had asked his foreman was, "Who does she belong to?" But now, in darkness, he asks a different question: "Who are you?"

Not What are you doing? Not Why are you here? Not who sent you, but who are you?

For the first time, Ruth answers with her name. Not the Moabite. Not the foreigner. Not the outsider.

Just Ruth.

"I am Ruth, your servant. Spread your covering over me." These words are Ezekiel's language, the corner of the garment, "KANAPH," the same word used for God spreading His covering over Israel: "I spread the corner of my garment over you and covered you..." (Ezekiel 16:8). For you are a redeemer. "For you are a 'go'el.'" A redeemer. A kinsman. One who has the right and the resources to buy back what was lost. Not offering herself but invoking the law. She requests redemption, not intimacy. Using the language of protection that he spoke over her in the field, under the sun, in front of his workers, he answers by saying, "My daughter."

In this moment, with these words, we see that Boaz is the same in the dark. If there was any doubt of his integrity and his character, it has now vanished. A line drawn against the darkness, ending any possibility of doubt that he would, or intends to, exploit this moment.

Chronicling her walk from Moab, he conveys that he views this act of kindness, this hesed, as her greatest act yet. What has stopped Ruth from choosing a younger man who could create a more promising future for her? A life free from the complications of Naomi's heritage and the burden of Levirate law? Placing herself in danger, standing in the gap for Naomi, making herself vulnerable, especially for her, with an already fragile reputation as a Moabite. Yet here she stands on the threshing floor, with courage and defiance, as she did on the road to Bethlehem, when she made that sacred, irrevocable vow to Naomi.

He knows that coming here took immense courage and his immediate response is to calm her fear. He gives her the only thing that is possible, under the law, that he can provide now—a promise. Made under stars, spoken in darkness. Spilling out words of honor over her, he tells her the entire town knows that she is "Eshet Chayil," the exact words used to convey the character of a Proverbs 31 woman. A woman of valor, of strength, of noble character. The female equivalent of what is said about Boaz: "ish gibbor chayil," a man of standing and strength.

DIVINE TIMING INSIGHT

We don't know how long it took Ruth to get the courage to follow through with her midnight mission. But we do know what it feels like to bolster the courage to do something challenging and vulnerable. More than likely, we delay, postpone, and procrastinate, and busy ourselves with prayers. While we're busy praying for a breakthrough, God is waiting for us to take the first step and do the thing that we fear the most. God waits for our active participation. He can't pour new life into the version of us that refuses to move. What if the very thing you're labeling as "too hard" is the door God is inviting you to walk through, to become who God is forming you to be?

TRACING YOUR OWN THREADS OF DIVINE TIMING

"My grace is sufficient for you, for my power is made perfect in weakness." (2 Corinthians 12:9)

> Are there actions I'm not taking because I'm afraid, or don't have what it takes? Is God giving me opportunities to build my strength that I'm not taking advantage of?

"Commit to the Lord whatever you do, and he will establish your plans." Proverbs 16:3

> What am I trying to do with my own limited reasoning, instead of asking for God's direction?

FILL-IN REFLECTION: STEPPING INTO THE UNKNOWN

A place where God is asking me to move, even without complete clarity:

____

____

____

____

The preparation I sense God inviting me into:

____

____

____

____

A place where I need protection and guidance:

DAY 17: RUTH 3:11-13

Now although it is true that I am a kinsman-redeemer, there is a closer redeemer than I. Stay here tonight, and in the morning if he wants to redeem you, that is good; let him redeem you. But if he is not willing, as surely as the LORD lives, I will redeem you. Lie here until morning (BSB)

For Ruth, the riskiest part may be behind her. But the plan isn't secure yet. Boaz knows something Ruth doesn't: there's another man, a closer relative, who has first claim to redeem Naomi's family land—and to marry Ruth. A lesser man might have hidden this. Boaz could have claimed Ruth immediately, bypassed the closer redeemer, and called it providence. After all, didn't Ruth come to him?

But Boaz won't cut corners, even if honesty costs him everything. He tells Ruth the truth: there's a closer redeemer who must be given the first option.

If Boaz had taken Ruth without honoring this right, the consequences would have been devastating. The closer redeemer could have contested the redemption—Naomi would remain homeless, her family's inheritance lost. Ruth's marriage would be legally questionable, and any children born to her wouldn't have clear claim to the family land.

And Ruth? After risking everything on the threshing floor, she wouldn't be remembered as a woman of noble character. She'd be the foreigner who seduced a man into an improper union. All the goodness Boaz saw in her—destroyed. All her courage—reframed as manipulation.

Even though desire and opportunity are right in front of him, Boaz takes no shortcuts and honors the rules God has put in place. He will give the closer redeemer first rights. His restraint becomes the very proof of his integrity, the type of righteousness that divine timing can trust.

When Boaz tells Ruth to stay until morning, he is threading a very small needle—balancing between two dangers. If she walks home in the night, she is vulnerable to attacks on her physical safety and her reputation. But leaving under the full sunrise also opens her to scandal. So, Ruth waits for the first grey light of dawn, "before one could recognize another" (Ruth 3:14). She leaves before the sun breaks the horizon—that threshold moment when there is just enough light to see the path you're walking on, but not enough to recognize a face from a distance.

Boaz doesn't yet know whether the closer redeemer will refuse. He's risking Ruth. He's risking his own hope. But he's ensuring that if redemption comes, it will come honestly. Dangerous in the way sacred risks are perilous. Vulnerable in the way faith can leave us exposed. And if you sit with it for just a moment, you realize how easily this could have ended differently. But Boaz proves to be the man his earlier words suggested. He honors her trust. Simple in its audacity. Beautiful in its risk. And quite remarkable in how it transforms vulnerability into victory.

DIVINE TIMING INSIGHT

Waiting isn't just about passing the time; it's a refining fire, shaping our character, stretching our trust, and preparing us for things we can't yet see. Transformation isn't only about receiving; it's about the slow, sacred work of the journey itself.

TRACING YOUR OWN THREADS OF DIVINE TIMING

"Better a patient person than a warrior, one with self-control than one who takes a city." (Proverbs 16:32)

> Am I trying to force an outcome rather than wait for God to open the right door?

"Suppose one of you wants to build a tower. Won't you first sit down and estimate the cost...?" (Luke 14:28)

> Do I tend to opt for the quick, easy fix? How do those events end up working out?

"Let integrity and uprightness protect me, because my hope, LORD, is in you." (Psalm 25:21)

Where is God inviting me to let integrity, rather than shortcuts, shape my choices?

FILL-IN REFLECTION

Where do I feel rushed:

____

____

____

A part of my life where I keep taking the easy road:

____

____

____

Areas where waiting feels uncomfortable but wise:

____

____

____

____

____

____

DAY 18: RUTH 3:14-18

So she lay down at his feet until morning, but got up before anyone could recognize another. Then Boaz said, "Do not let it be known that a woman came to the threshing floor." And he told her, "Bring me the shawl you are wearing and hold it out." When she did so, he poured into it six measures of barley and placed it on her. Then he went into the city. When Ruth returned to her mother-in-law, Naomi asked, "How did it go, my daughter?" Then Ruth told her everything Boaz had done for her. She said, "He gave me these six measures of barley, saying, 'Do not go back to your mother-in-law empty-handed.'" "Wait, my daughter," said Naomi, "until you find out how this matter turns out. For the man will not rest unless he has resolved the matter today" (BSB)

The threshing floor is a liminal space—a place between. Farmers come there in the gap between gathering and resting, between effort and reward. It's where the ground itself stands between public and private, where wheat and chaff are thrown into the air, and the wind decides what stays. It is the place where transformation happens. And now, in that thin window when night has not yet yielded to dawn, Ruth and Boaz wait. Two people waiting between promise and fulfillment. Two bearers of the covenant are waiting for the light to break.

Boaz gathers barley and pours it into Ruth's shawl—six measures. Six for now; the seventh is still coming. The rhythm of creation woven into a single gesture: six days of work, one day of rest. One measure of completion is held back in God's hand.

He sets the bundle across her shoulders. "Do not go back to your mother-in-law empty-handed." A mercy: Boaz remembers Naomi's words at the gate. "I went away full, but the LORD brought me back empty" (Ruth 1:21). He sends Ruth home with evidence that he intends to honor Ruth, but only when the time is right, and the covenant can begin.

When she receives the six measures, Naomi understands what Boaz intends. He is offering her a pledge. Now, they can only wait. Be still; the most challenging part of all. Ruth has walked the fifty miles, made her vow, and she has worked the fields and gleaned; there is nothing left for her to do; it is out of her hands. She must only trust now that the seventh measure, the completion, is still coming. Six measures now. The seventh is on its way.

DIVINE TIMING INSIGHT

In a sacred dance, God uses time to give us sometimes just enough evidence to offer hope, but not so much that we don't need faith. Dark moments like these, when there is nothing we can do, are precisely how God stretches our faith. Six measures of barley, not seven. The number that stands on the edge of completion, the day before Sabbath, the reminder that redemption has begun but isn't finished yet. Faith is built in the waiting.

TRACING YOUR OWN THREADS OF DIVINE TIMING

"Come to me... and I will give you rest." (Matthew 11:28–30)
> Where do you sense God inviting you to stop striving and begin trusting?

"The Lord will fight for you; you need only to be still." (Exodus 14:14)
> Where have you been trying to fix something that God could be asking you to place into His hands?

"But if we hope for what we do not yet have, we wait for it patiently."
(Romans 8:25)
> What unfinished place in your story is God asking you to wait on rather than push forward?

FILL-IN REFLECTION

The place where God is asking me to wait:

____

____

____

____

The "six measures" I already have:

____

____

____

Where I need to trust God to fight for me:

____

____

____

What I want to say to God as I wait:

____

____

____

____

____

____

____

____

____

____

____

____

DAY 19: RUTH 4:1-8

Meanwhile, Boaz went to the gate and sat down there. Just then the kinsman-redeemer he had mentioned came along, and Boaz said, "Come over here, my friend, and sit down." So he went over and sat down. Then Boaz took ten of the elders of the city and said, "Sit here," and they did so. And he said to the kinsman-redeemer, "Naomi, who has returned from the land of Moab, is selling the piece of land that belonged to our brother Elimelech. I thought I should inform you: Buy it back in the presence of those seated here and in the presence of the elders of my people. If you want to redeem it, do so. But if not, tell me, so I will know, because there is no one but you to redeem it, and I am next after you." "I will redeem it," he replied. Then Boaz said, "On the day you buy the land from Naomi, you must also acquire Ruth the Moabitess, the widow of the deceased, in order to raise up the name of the deceased on his inheritance." At this, the kinsman-redeemer said, "I cannot redeem it for myself, or I might jeopardize my own inheritance. Take my right of redemption, because I cannot redeem it." Now in former times in Israel, for the redemption and transfer of property to be legally binding, one party would remove his sandal and give it to the other. This was the method of legalizing transactions in Israel. So the kinsman-redeemer removed his sandal and said to Boaz, "Buy it for yourself" (BSB)

While Ruth waits, Boaz goes to the gate. Boaz rises with the purpose of a man who made a promise at midnight and intends to keep it by noon. He goes straight to the town gate, the public square where business, law, and community converge.

Just then, just as it happens in Ruth 2, the Scripture points us, again, humorously, to God's perfect timing; another "miqreh" (chance, happenstance) moment. Scripture's quiet wink at divine timing disguised as coincidence. It just so happens that the nearer kinsman is there. Boaz does not need to go searching for him; he's right here, at the exact moment Boaz must speak to him, as it happened. Again. God orchestrates every encounter needed for redemption to unfold. The right people appear at the right moments because God is directing the entire story, not just individual scenes.

His real name, the man Boaz refers to as "friend," never appears in the text. The Hebrew calls him "peloni almoni," the equivalent of "so-and-so." In a culture where names secure legacy and memory, his anonymity is not an oversight; it is prophecy. He is about to choose safety over sacrifice, self-protection over covenant, and Scripture will honor that choice with silence.

Boaz gathers ten elders, the minimum number required to bind legal action. So-and-so listens to the offer to redeem the land of Elimelek. The man calculates. Land means wealth. Land means expansion. Land means opportunity. "I will redeem it." (Ruth 4:4) Quick. Confident. Too simple. Boaz then reveals the second layer of the offer: "On the day you buy the land from Naomi, you also acquire Ruth the Moabite." (Ruth 4:5). With her comes responsibility. With her comes legacy work, not profit work. With her comes the duty to raise a son who will inherit Elimelek's land rather than his own sons. In his mind, the entire calculation pivots, and blessedly, falls apart. Cost now outweighs benefit. Risk now eclipses gain.

"Then I cannot redeem it because I might endanger my own estate." (Ruth 4:6). He refuses the responsibility. He protects his inheritance. He steps back from the sacrifice. He closes his fists around what is his, clinging to what he already has. In this act, he frees Boaz and saves himself from financial risk but forfeits what God might have given him.

To seal the deal, "so-and-so" removes his sandal. The sandal represents the right to walk the land as its rightful owner; to remove it is to surrender authority, to step aside so another may step forward. Moses removed his sandals before stepping onto holy ground (Exodus 3). When so-and-so takes off his sandal, he gives Boaz the right to step into the place, Elimelek's land, which so-and-so has abandoned. Sacred gestures, like this, of removing the sandal, seem trivial and odd. However, Scripture is full of strange, earthy customs; Abraham walking between the divided animals (Genesis 15), Jacob lifting a stone and pouring oil upon it (Genesis 28), and Jesus breaking bread and placing it into the hands of his disciples (Matthew 26).

And here, a sandal is placed in the hand of a redeemer, setting Ruth and Naomi free from their lives of desperation. And Ruth, through this transfer, steps into a destiny she never imagined. And redemption continues moving toward Bethlehem, toward

David, toward Christ. A foreign widow with nothing but loyalty becomes a matriarch in the line of the Messiah.

DIVINE TIMING INSIGHT

Redemption always asks for courage, sacrifice, selflessness, and integrity. It invites us to stand firm even when a more straightforward path lies open. In Ruth's story, every encounter is arranged with intention, even those that are obstacles. The unnamed man stands inches from an eternal legacy but steps back when the cost threatens his comfort. God doesn't avoid the messiness of redemption—He writes it into the center of His plan.

TRACING YOUR OWN THREADS OF DIVINE TIMING

"For where your treasure is, there your heart will be also." (Matthew 6:21)
> Where do I choose safety over sacrifice?

"What good will it be for someone to gain the whole world, yet forfeit their soul?" (Matthew 16:26)
> What am I protecting so tightly that it might be costing
> me something God is trying to give?

"Whoever loses their life for my sake will find it." (Matthew 10:39)
> Where is God inviting me to risk stepping into the story
> He is writing for me?

FILL-IN REFLECTION

What Am I Protecting?

____

____

____

The place where I am afraid to risk:

____

The sacrifice God might be inviting me to make:

____

____

____

____

What I need the courage to say yes to:

____

____

____

____

____

____

____

____

____

____

DAY 20: RUTH 4:9-12

At this time Boaz said to the elders and all the people, "You are witnesses today that I have bought from Naomi all that belonged to Elimelech, Chilion, and Mahlon. Moreover, I have acquired Ruth the Moabitess, Mahlon's widow, as my wife, in order to raise up the name of the deceased on his inheritance, so that his name will not disappear from among his brothers or from the gate of his home town. You are witnesses today." "We are witnesses," said all the people and elders at the gate. "May the LORD make the woman entering your home like Rachel and Leah, who together built the house of Israel. May you prosper in Ephrathah and be famous in Bethlehem. May your house be like the house of Perez, whom Tamar bore to Judah, through the offspring the LORD will give you by this young woman" (BSB)

So, Boaz takes Ruth. Not for gain, not for land, not to stretch his borders a smidgen wider; but only for the deliberate, costly work of redemption. He pays the full price on behalf of Naomi but gains nothing financially for a field that will never carry his name, for an inheritance that will slip from his hands.

The land will go to this son, a son who will be his by blood, but Mahlon's by law. A son rising in another man's line; a lineage Boaz will raise, nurture, and strengthen, but never claim.

This is the math of hesed: a love that spends itself; a love that signs its name on loss and still calls it covenant. He stands at the public gate, ten elders watching to solemnize the deal and make it legal, as he binds himself to a Moabite widow. Maybe he expects that murmurs will follow them, but Boaz is not a man governed by whispers. He has seen what others have missed: her courage, loyalty, a fierce and faithful heart that glows beneath the ashes of her loss. He takes her in because he sees God's fingerprints all over her story and refuses to let prejudice rewrite what heaven has already blessed.

He gains a wife; he gains a son. He gains a reputation carved from righteousness, not ambition. And he gives; he gives what cannot be returned, what he cannot claim for himself.

God has not given the child yet, but the elders still speak their blessings—names heavy with promise: Rachel, Leah, mothers who built Israel with longing and labor. And Tamar, like Ruth, was also a widow and an outsider who refused to vanish when doors were closed. Tamar, possibly a Canaanite, stands at Israel's beginning, and a Moabite here at its crown. Two women, both outsiders, stand at opposite ends of history, stitched together by bravery, by covenant love, by a God who builds His kingdom through those who risk everything when righteousness demands they do.

Behind Boaz's generosity lies Christ, the great Redeemer, stepping into our story and paying a price that restores an inheritance we squandered, absorbing a debt that brings Him no profit at all. We received the land. The name. The future. He gets the cross. Boaz is the whisper. Christ is the shout.

DIVINE TIMING INSIGHT

Divine timing does not always restore the life we expected, and if we had the choice, we will always choose God's something better than anything we can create on our own. His miracle is that he creates something new that could never have been made without the loss. God's divine timing weaves itself through legal negotiations and whispered blessings, through choices that resulted in payment from Boaz. God works in the unseen places, city gates, empty fields, conversations not meant for your ears; until suddenly the story breaks open, and you realize He has been restoring what was lost long before you recognized it needed resurrecting.

TRACING YOUR OWN THREADS OF DIVINE TIMING

"Whoever walks in integrity walks securely." (Proverbs 10:9).
Where is God inviting me to choose the secure path of integrity rather than the shortcut that tempts me?

"He who refreshes others will himself be refreshed." (Proverbs 11:25).
Boaz pours out what will not return to him, and God multiplies it beyond anything he could have built for himself.

"And we know that in all things God works for the good of those who love him." (Romans 8:28).

Where do I sense God working for my good even when the outcome is still invisible?

FILL-IN REFLECTION

A place where I sense God rebuilding something I thought was finished:

____

____

____

A sacrifice God is asking me to make that feels costly but holy:

____

____

____

A blessing I need to speak—before I see evidence, like the elders in Bethlehem:

____

____

____

____

____

____

____

DAY 21: RUTH 4:13-22

So Boaz took Ruth, and she became his wife. And when he had relations with her, the LORD enabled her to conceive, and she gave birth to a son. Then the women said to Naomi, "Blessed be the LORD, who has not left you this day without a kinsman-redeemer. May his name become famous in Israel. He will renew your life and sustain you in your old age. For your daughter-in-law, who loves you and is better to you than seven sons, has given him birth." And Naomi took the child, placed him on her lap, and became a nurse to him. The neighbor women gave him a name, saying, "A son has been born to Naomi." So they named him Obed. He was the father of Jesse, the father of David. Now these are the generations of Perez: Perez was the father of Hezron, Hezron the father of Ram, Ram the father of Amminadab, Amminadab the father of Nahshon, Nahshon the father of Salmon, Salmon the father of Boaz, Boaz the father of Obed, Obed the father of Jesse, and Jesse the father of David (BSB)

The moment he is born, the baby Obed gathers Naomi back into the story like a branch grafted to its original root. Too little to understand what his presence in the world means, yet his arrival, as a male, restores Elimelek's land and secures Naomi's future. With his birth, the property that once slipped into jeopardy returns to its rightful line, and Naomi, who crossed Bethlehem's threshold empty, now stands on land that will remain hers for life.

That day in Moab when her world collapsed—husband gone, sons gone, lineage severed- has now been redeemed. Boaz redeems Elimelek's land, paying for a field that will never enlarge his estate. He uses his resources to ensure it does not disappear from Elimelek's line. The land passes directly to Obed, legally Mahlon's son, heir to a man buried far from home. Boaz spends his own wealth to restore another man's name; his holdings diminish so another household can rise. "Menuchah." Rest. The rest that Naomi once sought for Ruth now settles onto her own life; a future rebuilt rather than replaced.

Boaz speaks aloud the names of Elimelek, Kilion, and Mahlon—three men whose graves lie in Moab, whose memory should have faded —and, in telling their names, he carries their legacy forward. What died in foreign soil is restored in covenant land. Elimelek, who fled from Bethlehem during the famine, now has a grandson born in Bethlehem. Mahlon, who left no heir, is named father to Obed. A line once severed is stitched back into Israel's story; a future that should have ended begins again.

The women of Bethlehem gather; the same women who once asked, "Can this be Naomi?" (Ruth 2:19) now recognize what has been restored. They call Obed the guardian-redeemer, the one who will sustain her in old age. His name means servant, quiet ruler, an early signal of the greater Servant who will one day come through this same line. Naomi holds the child, the same arms she once declared empty, and the lineage moves forward: Jesse, David, and eventually the birth in Bethlehem that will alter the world.

Her sorrow is not erased; it is reworked into something more substantial. Her bitterness is not dismissed; it is absorbed into redemption. The book closes with a genealogy, not as ornament, but as evidence. God keeps His promises across famine, funerals, foreign soil, and the unexpected faithfulness of outsiders. Restoration, in God's hands, is never the return of the old life, but the arrival of a future no one could have constructed from the ruins. Naomi hoped for survival; what she received was a place in the story that leads to Christ.

DIVINE TIMING INSIGHT

God's perfect timing isn't only about what He restores, but how He restores it. Naomi's story doesn't return to where it started; it grows into something her suffering could never have imagined. What once seemed like a random loss becomes the fertile ground where God plants a lineage. What appeared to be the end turns out to be the turning point for redemption. From famine to field, to threshing floor, and finally to the city gate, God arranges every step, not to recreate Naomi's past, but to reveal a future big enough to hold kings. Divine timing doesn't take shortcuts. It takes every sorrow, every risk, every cost, and weaves them into a restoration far greater than the pain that came before.

TRACING YOUR OWN THREADS OF DIVINE TIMING

"The LORD will fulfill his purpose for me." (Psalm 138:8)

Is there an area of my life where I need to ask God to restore purpose in something I thought was finished?

"Those who sow with tears will reap with songs of joy." (Psalm 126:5)
What loss is God transforming into future joy, even if I cannot yet see the harvest?

"From him and through him and for him are all things." (Romans 11:36)
Where is God working through circumstances I never would have chosen, weaving a story I could not have written?

FILL-IN REFLECTION

The place where God is restoring me in ways I did not expect:

____

____

____

____

The relationship or situation where God may be writing a new chapter:

____

____

____

____

The part of my story where I need to trust God's timing instead of my timeline:

____

____

____

____

The legacy I want my obedience to leave for the generations after me:

____

____

____

____

____

____

____

____

____

____

WHAT'S YOUR DIVINE TIMING STORY?

You've just read Ruth's journey from loss to redemption—but God is writing a story in your life too.

GRACE TRACKER:
COUNTING MY GRAINS OF GRACE

What if you began seeing your random moments as divine appointments? Ruth's story teaches us that God's hand is rarely clear in the moment, but it's always present. Use this tracker to record your grains of grace and start to see God's plan unfold in your life.

DATE	GOD'S GRACE

DATE	GOD'S GRACE

DATE	GOD'S GRACE

DATE	GOD'S GRACE

DATE	GOD'S GRACE

DATE	GOD'S GRACE

DATE	GOD'S GRACE

GOD'S DIVINE TIMING TIMELINE

GOD'S BEHIND-THE-SCENES PREPARATION IN RUTH

Before the Story Even Began - God's Preparation Through the Law:

God establishing the gleaning laws centuries earlier - In Leviticus 19:9-10 and Deuteronomy 24:19-21, God commanded landowners to leave the corners of fields unharvested and not gather all the grain, specifically providing for "the stranger, the fatherless, and the widow." This was written into the Law hundreds of years before Ruth needed it.

God instituting the kinsman-redeemer (go'el) system - Throughout the Law (Leviticus 25:25-55), God created the principle that a family member could redeem property and relatives, preserving family inheritance.

God establishing levirate marriage - In Deuteronomy 25:5-10, God provided the law that a brother should marry his deceased brother's widow to preserve the family name and inheritance, which informed the redemption customs in Ruth's time.

The combination of these laws —God uniquely positioned these legal provisions so that a poor, foreign widow would have both the right to survive (gleaning) and the possibility of full redemption (kinsman-redeemer), even though the laws didn't explicitly combine them as they do in Ruth's story.

Chapter 1 - Setting the Stage:

The famine in Bethlehem - God used this to drive Elimelek's family to Moab, where Ruth would eventually meet Mahlon and come to know the God of Israel

Boaz staying in Bethlehem during the famine - While Elimelek fled, Boaz remained faithful and stayed, positioning him to be Ruth's redeemer later.

The deaths of Elimelek, Mahlon, and Kilion - Though tragic, these deaths created the circumstances that would lead Ruth back to Bethlehem and to Boaz

Ruth's conversion and commitment to Naomi - God worked in Ruth's heart during her time in Moab, transforming a Moabite woman into a follower of Yahweh.

Naomi, hearing that "the LORD had visited His people by giving them bread" (Ruth 1:6), God ended the famine at precisely the right time.

Naomi's decision to return to Bethlehem - God prompted this return journey at precisely the right moment.

The timing of their arrival - "at the beginning of barley harvest" (Ruth 1:22) - They arrived when food was plentiful, and gleaning was available.

Chapter 2 - Divine Appointments:

Ruth knew about the gleaning laws - Somehow this Moabite woman learned about Israel's provision for the poor, showing God's preparation of her heart and mind.

Ruth "happening" to glean in Boaz's field (Ruth 2:3) - The text says "her hap was to light on" Boaz's field, emphasizing what appeared to be chance but was divine orchestration.

Boaz's presence in the fields that very day - He arrived from Bethlehem at just the right time to notice Ruth

Boaz's godly character was already being established - God had been preparing a man of integrity, wealth, and faith to be the redeemer.

Boaz, being a landowner who honored the gleaning laws, went beyond the minimum requirements.

The foreman's positive report about Ruth - God gave Ruth favor in the eyes of the workers before Boaz even spoke to her

Boaz, being a close relative/kinsman-redeemer, God's genealogical positioning placed Boaz in the exact family line needed.

Boaz's immediate kindness and protection - God moved his heart to go beyond the law's requirements in caring for Ruth.

Chapter 3 - The Redemption Plan:

Naomi's wisdom in guiding Ruth - God gave Naomi insight into the customs and the right timing for Ruth's appeal.

Naomi, understanding the kinsman-redeemer system, knew the legal pathways available and how to pursue redemption.

The threshing floor timing - After the harvest was complete, when Boaz would be in good spirits and accessible.

Boaz's integrity in the nighttime encounter - God had prepared his character to respond honorably.

Boaz immediately understood Ruth's request for redemption - His familiarity with the law and willingness to act.

The existence of a closer kinsman-redeemer - God had even prepared a "backup plan" to ensure everything was done properly.

Chapter 4 - The Public Redemption:

Boaz immediately goes to the gate - Divine urgency and timing.

The closer relative appearing at the gate - Perfect timing for the legal transaction.

The closer relative's willingness to redeem the land initially - Showing the system was working as designed.

The closer relative's withdrawal when he learned that marrying Ruth was part of the redemption - Clearing the path for Boaz (possibly because it would complicate his own inheritance)

The elders and witnesses are present - Community confirmation of God's plan.

The legal transaction being conducted properly according to the Law - God's laws provided the framework for legitimate redemption.

The blessing pronounced by the elders invoking Rachel, Leah, and Tamar - Prophetic blessing pointing to Ruth's place in redemptive history.

The birth of Obed - God's gift of a son to continue the line.

Obed becoming the grandfather of David - The ultimate revelation that God was preparing the Davidic line and ultimately the lineage of Jesus Christ

Overarching Divine Providence:

The preservation of Elimelek's family name and line - Despite all three men dying, God ensured continuation through the very laws He had established

Including a Moabite woman in the Messianic line - Demonstrating God's grace extends beyond Israel.

Transforming Naomi's bitterness into blessing - From "call me Mara" to being a nurse for the child who would grandfather a king.

The entire story occurred during the dark days of the Judges - God working His redemptive purposes even in Israel's worst spiritual period.

The laws God gave Moses centuries earlier being perfectly suited - The gleaning laws and redemption laws worked together to save Ruth and Naomi, showing God's foreknowledge.

The genealogy ending with David (Ruth 4:18-22) - Revealing that this entire story was God preparing the way for Israel's greatest king and ultimately for Jesus, the King of Kings

THEOLOGICAL THEMES
THROUGH HEBREW TERMS

HEBREW TERMS GLOSSARY
KEYWORDS & THEOLOGICAL CONCEPTS

1. HESED (חֶסֶד)

Transliteration: kheh-SED

Literal meaning: Covenant love, loyal kindness, steadfast love

Theological significance: Covenant faithfulness; love that overflows beyond duty or obligation

Cross-references: Psalm 136; Ruth 1:8, 2:20, 3:10

2. MENUCHAH (מְנוּחָה)

Transliteration: meh-noo-KHAH

Literal meaning: Rest, resting place, settled peace

Theological significance: Not mere physical rest but a place of belonging, security, and settled peace; home in the fullest sense

Cross-references: Ruth 1:9, 3:1; Ruth 3:18

3. GO'EL (גֹּאֵל)

Transliteration: go-EL

Literal meaning: Kinsman-redeemer, next of kin, rescuer

Theological significance: A family member with both the right and responsibility to buy back property, marry a widow, or restore what was lost; points to Christ as the ultimate Redeemer

Cross-references: Ruth 2:20, 3:9, 3:12, 4:1-6; Leviticus 25:25-55; Job 19:25; Isaiah 59:20

4. TACHAT KENAFAV (תַּחַת כְּנָפָיו)

Transliteration: TAH-khat keh-nah-FAV

Literal meaning: Under his wings

Theological significance: Ancient covenant language of protection and refuge under God's care; image of a bird sheltering chicks

Cross-references: Psalm 91:4; Ruth 2:12; Matthew 23:37; Deuteronomy 32:11

5. ESHET CHAYIL (אֵשֶׁת חַיִל)

Transliteration: EH-shet khah-YEEL

Literal meaning: Woman of valor, woman of strength/substance

Theological significance: A woman of excellence, strength, and godly character; connects Ruth to the Proverbs 31 woman

Cross-references: Ruth 3:11; Proverbs 31:10-31

7. GER (גֵּר)

Transliteration: GEHR

Literal meaning: Stranger, sojourner, foreigner, resident alien

Theological significance: A foreigner who has aligned with Israel's God and community; entitled to legal protection under the gleaning laws

Cross-references: Ruth 1:16-17; Leviticus 19:9-10, 23:22; Deuteronomy 24:19-22

WHAT'S YOUR DIVINE TIMING STORY?

You've walked with Ruth from loss to redemption—and God is weaving something in your life too.

Where are you on His timeline?

The Divine Timing Evidence Log is a free tool to help you:

Identify which of the Seven Stations you're in

- Notice how God has already been preparing you

- Spot patterns of His faithfulness

- Move forward with clarity and hope

When you begin to trace God's fingerprints, faith becomes steadier and stronger.

Grab your Divine Timing Log at susiej.com/timing or scan the QR Code.

And, I would be ever so grateful to hear from you in your review!